Mission Miracles

and the

Prayers of
God's People

ELEANOR FIOL

ISBN 978-1-0980-6464-8 (paperback)
ISBN 978-1-0980-6465-5 (digital)

Christian Faith Publishing, Inc.
832 Park Avenue
Meadville, PA 16335
www.christianfaithpublishing.com

Printed in the United States of America

Contents

DEDICATION

Often as we traveled around and visited churches as missionaries, the thought came to mind, "The work these dear people are doing looks more difficult than what we do. Missions committees and faithful supporters try hard to convince preoccupied people to be interested in missions, dealing with all of the details involved in holding a missions conference, trying to visualize where their missionaries (sometimes dozens of them) are working, what they are doing and what their lives must be like, reading all of the letters, trying to get other people to read the correspondence, and on top of that, thinking of ways to get people to come for one more meeting a week/month where they will spend time praying for missions. My heart goes out to them.

It should be said right here, however, that on the positive side, I have been impressed with the diligence in most of the churches we go to with which missionaries are prayed for in an informed way in some of the worship services.

We found a wonderful example of what we seemed to have lost in many churches that left us in awe when David and I drove north, across the border to Canada. There is a church in Nova Scotia that has been supporting for many years the children's home we worked with. We felt they deserved a visit, and we were right.

The adult Sunday school class had been praying for and giving to the home since—well, they didn't remember when exactly, but those who now were in their seventies and eighties were in the youth group when they started.

Also there was the Catherine Ferguson Missionary Society. I had seen their name for years on the printouts of donors and wondered who they were. I learned during my meeting with them on a Monday morning that Catherine Ferguson was a missionary to Africa for many years who was from their church. She was now with the Lord.

They talked about having started their group and interest in missions in the junior missionary society when they were young people. Now they were 70 and above. Praying for many missionaries as well as the children's home in which we worked had held together their fellowship for at least fifty years. I delighted in telling them what I knew of the work they had prayed for and sat in awe at such life-long faithfulness. No wonder we have seen so many dedicated young people who grew up in the home serving the Lord and sharing their faith. No wonder the Lord has protected the work time and time again.

I remember being impressed with the relationship my mother-in-law had with a certain Sunday school class and a particular "women's circle" from one of their supporting churches. It was a lovely thing to see her sitting up nights on the field, writing long letters to them (by hand), treasuring their prayer support and friendship. Such friends saw her and her husband and family through many trying times.

And after a lifetime of missions, I myself can list a number of groups, women's groups or mixed, and many churches with whom we have had such a relationship for years. Of all of the numerous things we are thankful for as we review our ministry, such praying, supporting friends are high on the list.

Some churches assigned missionaries to elders' groups or K groups. Some formed separate groups to pray for missions. Some systematically covered all of the missionaries and fields at mid-week prayer meetings or worship services. Many individuals also served as prayer warriors privately.

Whatever the method, we thank you. Your contribution to the spread of Christ's Kingdom around the world is inestimable. This book is dedicated to you.

Author's Note

When I was leading Bible study groups for women, especially new believers, I would warn the students before we started on a topic such as the Trinity or the two natures of Christ in one person or a sovereign God allowing us to have free will. I would say, *"Now don't think you are going to be able to fully understand how this can be. Our minds are finite. God is infinite. We are not capable of completely comprehending God and his thoughts (Isaiah 55:8,9). But we are going to see what He has revealed to us in His Word and do our best to understand and to obey."*

Lately, I have come to see that there is another truth that should be introduced in that way. It is the importance of our prayer in the light of the sovereignty of God.

I heard a pastor explain it so nicely recently by saying, *"God 'programs' our prayers into his sovereignty/plans."*

We pray because Christ taught us to pray and because Christ Himself set the example.

The New Testament writers indicated that the prayers of believers had an important part in their ministries as well as in the lives of others:

> *The effective prayer of a righteous man can accomplish much.* (James 5)

> *For I know that this will turn out for my deliverance through your prayer—and the supply of the Spirit of Jesus Christ.* (Phil. 1:19)

Therefore I exhort first of all that supplications, prayers, intercessions and giving of thanks be made for all men. (1 Tim. 2:1)

He rescued us from such great danger of death, and he will continue to rescue us; in Him we have put our hope (that) He will also rescue us again, as you help us with prayer, so that thanks may be given by many on our behalf for the gift granted us through the prayers of many. (2 Cor. 1:10–11)

But, meanwhile, also prepare a guest room for me, for I trust that through your prayers I shall be granted to you. (Philemon 22)

Praying always with all prayer and supplication in the Spirit, being watchful to this end with all perseverance and supplication for all the saints—And for me, that utterance may be given to me, that I may open my mouth boldly to make known the mystery of the gospel. (Ephesians 6:18, 19)

Now that my husband and I are officially retired, we find ourselves on the other side of the prayer letters—the receiving side rather than the sending side. We have always been grateful for the prayers of the people of God among our family, friends, and churches. We have known all along that the work God has done has been very little of us and very much of God's Spirit and the prayers of God's people. And we have been so grateful to have a small part in it and to have the support of the prayers of God's people.

But what we didn't fully realize before we retired is how hard Satan works to keep those prayers from going up on the receiving side of the prayer letters. So I hope that this book may be an encouragement and help to individuals and groups who are concerned for God's work around the world and want to have an important part in it through *prayer.*

Recently I heard a presentation by a PCA pastor who had been on the mission field teaching pastors. He showed a picture of a group of believers and explained with some amazement that after his teaching session, these people wanted to have a prayer meeting!!

Those who are on the front lines where the Holy Spirit is moving in new territories report that new believers know how important prayer meetings are and want to have them. They seem to realize that as they have received a wonderful revelation from God in His Word, they should respond by praising and praying it back to Him. They know that though they pray individually they also need the presence of other believers in prayer fellowship. They know that it is a wonderful way to bear one another's burdens (Gal. 6:2).

In the excitement of the resurrection and anticipation of the advance of the church and in the face of persecution, early believers were found together in prayer. We too are living in a time of great advancement in the kingdom of God around the world, coupled with severe persecution of Christians. Shouldn't we, like them, be gathering together in prayer?

I heard a man tell of when he was traveling in Nepal and needed a place to sleep one night. He was allowed to go into a church and spread his bed roll on a bench. Imagine his surprise and embarrassment when early in the morning, he awoke to find himself in the middle of a prayer meeting. Every day, early in the morning, the believers would meet together for prayer before they went to work. And in many cases, it meant a long walk for them.

It seems to me there are several reasons why it is especially hard for us in North America to attend group prayer meetings. Let me list some of them for you.

1. *We are a culture of individuals and feel that it is enough for us to pray privately.*

    Of course, our prayers in our closets are important. And we should not pray publicly in order to show off our ability to pray as the Pharisees often did (Matt. 6:5, 6). But which one of us can honestly say we spend enough time in serious prayer by ourselves? I certainly can't.

The fact that the model prayer the Lord gave us in Matthew 6 uses a plural adjective (Our Father) would seem to indicate the importance of group prayers.

I personally have found that engaging in group prayer has enhanced my private prayer life. There is a special dynamic in praising the Lord, thanking Him, and making our petitions *"where two or three are gathered together"* with Christ in their midst (Matt. 18:20). And I learn much from hearing the prayers of others.

Christ wanted Peter, James, and John to watch with him in his hour of trial, but they fell asleep—*twice* (Matt. 26:37–46). Are we sleeping when we think that it is not important for us to bear each other's burdens in group prayer and to bear the burden of Christ for the world?

2. *Women may not be given responsibility to lead in prayer in worship services and therefore may not feel comfortable praying out loud.*

There is no prohibition in Scripture for women leading in prayer in small groups or even in large ones as far as I can see, and we should have opportunity to develop that social skill as we do other abilities. Praying out loud is a gift for each one of us that needs to be practiced and developed, not only by women but by all believers. In teaching new believers on the mission field, it is considered important for them to learn to pray audibly in the presence of other believers and even with those who are not believers who are usually happy for people to pray for their needs. It is an opportunity for unbelievers to hear the Gospel and see the power of God. Praying out loud is an important testimony of our faith.

3. *People don't like to have to pray long prayers after a whole line of other people have already prayed long prayers.*

I agree with that viewpoint and really believe that small group prayer meetings should be conducted in a conversational, more relaxed way. It requires perseverance and patience to find ways to change the old patterns, but there are many ways it can be done.

A group may agree to pray short prayers on one subject. Each person is expected to contribute only a sentence or two on that subject, though he or she can pray short prayers any number of times. A pause can be taken to discuss the next subject for prayer. A little thoughtful experimentation should come up with a way that a group will feel comfortable, and every person will feel actively engaged. It will take determination and practice, but it will be well worth the effort.

It seems that sometimes when we gather together in His name, we completely ignore Him and talk only to each other, though He is right there with us. We may have brief opening and closing prayers. Perhaps we should address the Lord more in our gatherings and each other less.

One of the most meaningful prayer meetings I have attended was with a group of ladies in India. That day we chose to pray for each of us one at a time. We heard one person's concerns and then prayed for her, each one praying a sentence or two once or many times. Then we went on to the next.

4. *People lead busy lives.*
    Women are diligent in looking after their homes and children, leading or attending Bible studies, doing charitable work, visiting the sick, sending some of their number on mission trips, organizing regional meetings, etc. Men are busy at their careers, taking responsibility for the families, leading the church, etc. The list is endless, and I greatly admire and approve of all of it. Some people tend to think that having a meeting for "just prayer" is a waste of time.

    But as we are careful to remember that we are not saved by works but by grace, so we should be aware that works will not increase our faith and spiritual maturity in the same way that prayer and dependence on the Holy Spirit will. Too many works without prayer can put us in the position of working in the flesh rather than in the Spirit. Our works must flow out of our faith enhanced by prayer. Prayer is our way of acknowledging our dependence on the grace of God. It is every bit as important as Bible study or good works and worth holding meetings for its own sake.

5. *Western culture tends to be more task-oriented than people-oriented.*
    And we need our "space," our time to ourselves after we have finished our work. Often there is little time left for spiritual meetings. But we need relationships—with God and with fellow believers, and prayer is all about just that. We must make time.
    People in South Asia don't seem to need "*space.*" Being alone is a frightening thing for them. When my husband went away overnight, their eyes would get wide with terror as they realized that I would be "*alone?*" Well—the landlord and his family lived in the apartment upstairs. On any three sides of our ground floor apartment, at night I could be awakened to find myself part of a sending-off party or an argument at a neighbor's house; neighbors' houses were very close. But I was not in the same room with those people and they weren't my relatives, so I was "alone." Being alone is something they rarely feel a need for, and actually fear.
    People in that culture may or may not have a relationship with God, but they know the value of their relationships with each other.

But this is not a book merely demonstrating the importance of prayer. It is a series of chapters giving abbreviated biographies of missionaries of the past to demonstrate how friends and supporters should be praying for missionaries of today.
Use it as a tool to help you as you pray, alone or in groups, for your missionaries, that you may have some discernment in "read-

ing between the lines" and praying for matters that missionaries do not feel free to write about in prayer letters or may only hint at. It may help you to increase your prayers rather than decrease them when you don't hear from a missionary. I used to say, "Remember, when you don't hear from us, it means we need *more* prayer, not less."

The title, *Mission Miracles*, is borrowed from a book by my mother-in-law, Esther Fiol, *Mission Miracles, Memoirs of Frank and Esther Fiol, the Early Years and Ministry in Kanpur.* My husband, David's mother, called every work of the Lord that she saw in her family a "miracle." David's life as a boy prompted a number of references to miracles as he came near to death several times through illness or boyish pranks. Indeed, since I have known him as an adult, the Lord has had to perform a number of "miracles" in his life. But that is for another book.

I recommend that you read the full biographies of the missionaries mentioned in this book. In addition to the works referred to in the footnotes, there are multiple books available on the lives of many of these missionaries. Several good series to have in your church library, where young people should be encouraged to use them, are *Heroes of the Faith, Christian Heroes Then and Now, (put out by YWAM), Men of Faith, and Women of Faith.* All can be easily found by searching the web.

The missionaries whose stories are told in this book are from various backgrounds and denominations, but they have one goal in common. Their main desire is to see that the message of the Gospel of Jesus Christ is delivered to all nations. This Gospel, or good news, according to the Word of God, is that whosoever will repent of his sins and believe that Jesus Christ, the Son of God, came into the world to give His life to pay the penalty for his/her sins and rise from the dead will be saved. He/she will be made a new creation and will spend eternity with the Lord.

May this little book be used to encourage groups or individuals in praying for missions at home and around the world. Perhaps you will want to read one chapter at the beginning of each prayer meeting or personal prayer time.

Or may it be a blessing in being read just like any other book as it describes how God has been working and is still working to build His kingdom around the world through the prayers of God's people.

For easy reference, I have collected the prayer requests at the end of each chapter into one chapter at the end of the book titled as "Prayer Requests."

CHAPTER I
~ ~ Nothing New Under the Sun ~ ~

William Carey

One of my hobbies is reading missionary biographies. I have been greatly inspired by reading about God's use of people in the past who have answered the call to go into all the world with the Gospel.

A number of years ago, copies of some old letters came into my hands. They were written by a young woman named Annie who was a missionary in the last half of the nineteenth century in Asia, where we lived and worked for the last thirty-one years of our ministry. Annie and her family lived near the grounds where one of the institutions in which we worked is located. She established a school in that location that is a large Christian institution still today. As far as I know, no biography has been written of her short life, though she and her husband are briefly mentioned in some reports of their mission.

Annie and I had many things in common. Each of us was with a Presbyterian mission, was from Pennsylvania, was married, had three children, and helped to establish a school that is functioning to this day.

I felt a kinship with Annie in all of those areas, though her life had been harder in many respects. She had arrived on a sailing boat after four months at sea while we had made the trip on ocean liners in one month. She had longed for letters from her family, which took months to arrive while I have enjoyed instant e-mail in recent years. She died of Hepatitis in her mid-twenties. I recovered from the same disease in 1984 in my mid-forties to live on. But still we have much in common, and I found it inspiring to read of her life. The Gospel we are proclaiming never changes, and God's command to all of His people to proclaim it is always the same. God's ways of dealing with His servants and building His kingdom don't really vary much it seems from age to age. Truly I came to realize that there is *nothing new under the sun* as the preacher declares in Ecclesiastes. Actually, all believers have most, if not all, of these issues that we are looking at in missionaries in common with each other as we follow the Lord.

Most of us, when thinking of the history of missions, will remember William Carey. While rereading his biography, I was again struck by how much servants of the Lord today have in common with those of all ages.

William Carey was, as you know, one of the first British missionaries to serve in India. When he sailed for Calcutta in 1793, facing a perilous trip of almost five months, he had already earned himself the title of the Father of Modern Missions. As a successful Baptist pastor who was instrumental in reviving two churches, he had been responsible for convincing twenty-four Baptist churches of the Northampton Baptist Association to which he belonged to establish a mission society, most likely the first in England.

His pamphlet, "An Enquiry into the Obligations of Christians to Use Means for the Conversion of the Heathens, in Which the Religious State of the Different Nations of the World, the Success of Former Undertakings and the Practicability of Further Undertakings are Considered"_(or *Enquiry* for abbreviation) was used, along with his preaching and arguments, to change the minds of the hyper-Calvinists of his church. They are remembered for John Ryland's rebuke of William at a meeting, "Young man, sit down. If God wants to convert the heathen, He will do it without consulting you or me."[1]

It is interesting to note that John Ryland soon became one of his staunchest supporters and an officer of the first missionary society.

The fact was that God *had already* "consulted" William Carey, has called many others since, and has sent them forth to build His Church.

In a sermon preached at the meeting where a decision was made to appoint the committee to form a missionary society, William preached on Isaiah 54, "Enlarge the place of thy tent—" and ended with the famous statement, "Brothers, expect great things from God. Attempt great things for God."[2]

In the last section of *Enquiry*, William wrote, "Every Christian must pray. God will answer. And besides praying, Christians must 'plod and plan'. Societies must be formed—then 'stout hearts' must volunteer. Then all the Christians in the congregation must fund them."[3] Every word is applicable to missions today.

Most mission agencies and missionaries follow the guidelines set down by Carey in his book. How grateful we are for all of the plodding, planning, and praying done by our sending agency, and the churches and individuals who have backed us and the Lord's work in Asia. We were spared many of the problems that William Carey experienced.

William's Society certainly did pray, plod, and plan. They raised enough money to send him and John Thomas and their families to India, even though some of the people in those twenty-four churches were very poor. They prayed and were supportive, even though it took six months for letters to go one way. They sent two more batches of missionaries in William's lifetime, and especially the first batch was made up of people who were exactly those needed at precisely the right time.

---

[1] William Carey, *Father of Modern Missions by Sam Wellman*, (Uhrichsvillle, OH: Barbour Publishing, Inc.), p. 57

[2] Ibid. p. 62

[3] Ibid. pp. 59–60

The Society first appointed Dr. John Thomas, a medical doctor, who knew Bengali and had experience in evangelism in Bengal. John told them that two educated Indians of the Brahmin caste had made an appeal for someone to help them translate the Word. William quickly volunteered to go as John's assistant since his interest and abilities lay in the area of translation. William was now thirty-one. John was around thirty-eight.

William's wife, Dolly, was terrified of going to India, as much for William as for herself. William had almost died of a fever, which had taken its toll on his hair as well as his health. It also had taken the life of their first baby, a little girl.

He and Dolly agreed that he would go himself with their oldest son, Felix, for three years and then come back and consider if the rest of the family should go. She was pregnant with their fourth son when William and John and his family were due to sail to India. But they were delayed and at the last minute, after the baby was born, John and William talked her into taking the children and going with them. Dolly's consolation was that her sister, Kitty, was willing to go along to be her companion.

Even before their ship left the harbor, John confessed what the mission board's investigation of him had not uncovered. He was in debt to many people, both in Calcutta and London. That was perhaps one of the reasons he had traveled between London and Calcutta as ship's doctor on several voyages, to avoid debtors on both sides. He was an impetuous and convincing person, inclined to make promises he could not fulfill.[4]

On the voyage, John and William confessed their faults to one another. John revealed that he had been a "wild boy; had many debts; lost many friends thru hard words in self-righteousness and enthusiasm." William confessed to being "dead in spirit and despairing often. How can I expect to be of any use to the heathen with such barrenness in my own soul?" John's conclusion was, "We perfectly complement each other; I soar too high; you soar too low."

---

[4] William Carey, *Father of Modern Missions by Sam Wellman*, (Uhrichsvillle, OH: Barbour Publishing, Inc.), pp 61–89

After their arrival in India, John and William engaged in evangelism a little over a month before John put his energies into setting up a medical practice in Calcutta to support his family and the work. He had told the board that missionaries could support themselves, and they were already running out of money. The money that was raised was enough for passage and only one month's expenses for all of them, and the goods that they had brought with them to sell did not bring as much money as they had hoped.

Around the same time, Dolly and Felix came down with the "bloody flux," a bad form of diarrhea, which was treated with the use of leaches to suck the blood. The complaining of Kitty and Dolly, which had started on the long, stormy sea voyage, continued. William was left wondering what to do next as they were temporarily quartered in the Portuguese settlement of Bandel. He no longer had the experienced Dr. Thomas with whom to consult.

He had heard of free land being given away in the Sunderbans, east of Calcutta, and decided to settle there. They were soon to find out that the Sunderbans were considered the least desirable place to live in all of India. They would have to travel through crocodile-infested rivers to even get there. The area was famous for man-eating tigers, poisonous snakes, and mysterious deadly diseases. But it was too late to stop the plan. They struck out for the Sundarbans in February 1794.

Both Dolly and Kitty were constantly complaining and blaming William for all of their problems. (Perhaps it should be a warning for us to note that complaining and blaming ended up in insanity for Dolly). A constant source of irritation to the two women was the fact that Thomas and his family had been living in a comfortable house in Calcutta, while they had ended up in this dreadful place.

To make matters worse for Dolly, Kitty fell in love with the East India Co. officer, Charles Short, who was their host during the time they were in the Sundarbans. The two married, robbing Dolly of her companion. Charles died five or six years later of a disease contracted in that dangerous place, and Kitty returned to England.

William proceeded to build a bamboo house on their property and plant a garden. He was also a botanist and did much work in that field in India. Their land was some distance (in a lonely place) from Charles Short's house. Dolly continued to complain and prayed that God would take them from that place. Her prayers were answered when they received a letter from Thomas saying that after learning what a dreadful place they had chosen, he had arranged for William as well as himself to each manage an indigo plantation. That meant they would live in comfortable houses in a relatively safe area and would have a steady income as well as freedom to evangelize the people working for them.

Thomas sent money for William and his family to leave that place, so by the end of May, before the rains started, they had traversed the river again and settled at Mudnabati on an indigo plantation.[5]

After that rainy season, which was the busiest on an indigo plantation, in September, William came down with fever. George Udny happened to visit and was able to diagnose what they called "jungle fever" (most likely malaria) and administer "bark" (quinine). William recovered from malaria and soon contracted what was probably cholera with which five-year-old Peter also was afflicted. William again recovered. Peter did not.

Then followed the nightmare of getting someone to help bury the child. Neither Hindus nor Muslims, both of whom lived in the area, would build a box, dig a grave, or carry the body for these foreigners. The four men who finally agreed to be hired to dig the grave, which had to be far away from the Muslim graves, were banished from their village by the Headman. William threatened the Headman with action by the British authorities, which caused him to change his mind.

Though William had hoped Dolly would improve in a new situation, her complaining turned into insanity. She began to accuse William openly in public of having affairs with other women. Then

---

she began attacking him physically and trying to kill him. At other times, she would seem completely sane and reasonable.

The Thomases came to assess the situation. Soon they were convinced that it was Dolly and not William who was insane. It helped them understand when she started accusing Mrs. Thomas of having an affair with William. The doctor recommended that she be restrained in a room for William's safety. When William revealed that Dolly was pregnant again, the doctor advised them to wait until after the baby was born, in hopes that the delivery would improve her mental health.

The birth of the baby did not help and soon after Dolly made an attempt on William's life again. She was then confined to her room with baby Jonathan and eventually had to be tied down. William, Dolly, and the children endured this until they had been in India for fourteen years, and people got used to hearing her ravings when they came to their home. Dolly died of a slow "lung fever" that silenced her and finally took her life in 1807. William said sadly, "How she suffered. At last she has found peace with the Lord."[6]

Did the people of the sending churches in England know how much Dolly suffered? Did their prayers focus on resisting the work of the devil in her life? Mail took a matter of months to reach its destination if all went well. Were any of the missionaries even inclined to write of these problems or was it not considered appropriate to mention such things? We don't know. No doubt people were praying for the success of the work, but did they have any idea of the cost?

The Marshmans and Wards were two of five couples who were sent to join the Careys and Thomases in 1799. Soon after they arrived, Hannah Marshman took the four Carey boys in hand and managed them. Joshua, her husband, an educator who was to establish many schools for children, and William Ward, the printer, also helped William raise his boys. Three of the boys became missionaries in Asia. The youngest became a lawyer in India.

---

[6] Ibid. p. 178

God, in His wonderful providence, put all things together to start the work in Serampore in 1799 when the new missionaries arrived. This was six years after the arrival of the Careys and the Thomases. Much translation had been done but not printed. The entire Bible in Bengali was almost ready. Through all of the harsh trials that had come their way and other efforts of the enemy to thwart the work they had come to do, Carey had continued translating the Word.

Within a few months, an amazing set of circumstances came together. A type foundry that would make type for all of the vernaculars of India was being set up by the authorities in Calcutta. An officer of the East India Company donated a press; one of the new missionaries was a printer; William was forced to leave the Indigo plantation because of drought; and the new missionaries had to land in Serampore, which was a Danish colony, and stay there since the British wouldn't have them. While the new governor of Calcutta was anti-missionary and refused admittance to them, the Danish governor in Serampore entreated them to take asylum there, set up their press, and start a church in his house and a school in his buildings.

Thus a work started at Serampore that continued until William Carey's death in 1834 and beyond and had a lasting impact throughout the land of India in more ways than we can count and to an extent that would be hard to measure.[7]

John Thomas did not join the mission at Serampore where in 1799, five women, five men, and nine children began living together in a very large house on two acres, shared a common dining room, and built on the work that had been started by John and William. William was their leader now, though he insisted, "We have only one master: Christ."

By that time, John had left his indigo plantation. When he returned to visit at the mission on their day of thanksgiving, he looked unhinged; his activities were more desperate than ever. William suspected he might be involved in the rum trade. He had signs of mental

---

[7] William Carey, *Father of Modern Missions by Sam Wellman*, (Uhrichsvillle, OH: Barbour Publishing, Inc.), pp. 147–173

illness, and he had a vacant look in his eyes. It is possible that he was suffering from what we today call manic depression. He left again.

Seven years after William's and John's arrival the first person came to Christ. It was Dr. John Thomas who led Krishna Pal, the Hindu carpenter, to the Lord. John was called to Serampore to set Krishna's dislocated shoulder and was used to open his eyes to the Gospel. William thought at the time that Thomas still did not look well.

John, a keen evangelist (among other things), had labored fifteen years and William, seven, to see this moment. They were overjoyed when others also soon came to the Lord. But at the time of Krishna's baptism in December 1800, Thomas had to be restrained in his madness and could not attend. He left them again and died of cholera in October 1801, at the age of about forty-five. William was still calling him his "dear friend," though at times it had seemed he was his worst enemy. William was in his late thirties by that time.[8]

What can we glean from this information that will help us understand present-day missionaries (or servants of the Lord anywhere for that matter)?

William's wife, Dorothy "Dolly" Carey, suffered much as the family member of a missionary. While she evidently supported William's ministry through the trials and poverty that they experienced when he was a pastor in England, she did not hold up under the hardships, sorrows, and dangers they faced in India. In these days, mission boards are cautious if a spouse does not feel a call that the husband or wife does. Even though the call and dedication may be the same in the beginning, things may change later on.

"Spouses and children must be remembered and encouraged. They sometimes suffer in unique ways and don't always understand why. They miss their husbands/fathers who often must leave them for periods of time for their work, which puts an extra burden on the wives/mothers. They sometimes don't have friends of their own culture and don't understand those of the host culture. They may feel they are missing things they would enjoy in their home country".

---

[8] Ibid. pp. 147–164

Families of missionaries often feel that they do not have a choice in matters. As our own children grew older, we were careful to allow them to be part of the decision-making process. When I asked our daughter if she would like us to leave the field when she was starting college in the United States, she was shocked that I would suggest such a thing. "No, we are a missionary family," was her immediate response. But we felt she should have the chance to express a choice.

There will be times when some missionary children may feel that their opportunities for education or other areas of their lives were harmed by their parents' work. Missionaries cannot always write such things in their prayer letters except perhaps in very vague terms.

PRAY...

- ...for your missionaries' most serious trials and temptations, those they cannot express in letters. Pray that God will answer their prayers though they may not be free to reveal them to supporters.
- ...for the mission agencies, churches, and individuals who support them, that they will know how to pray, will take the time to do it, and will know what else they should do.
- ...that all family members will sense God's leading and mature in their spiritual lives as a result of the work to which their families have been called. Get to know each family member of your missionaries and pastors, and their circumstances, and pray for each one regularly.
- ...for single missionaries who have families at home. Perhaps those families are concerned about their loved ones being on the field while single. The families at home, of both single and married missionaries, need prayer. Also intercede for your missionary's coworkers that they will prove to be caring brothers and sisters in the Lord and will always look out for each other.
- ...that the Lord will enable your missionaries and their families to be inspired by the stories of others and to grow

in the faith that God uses difficulties, evil, and *all things* to accomplish His good purposes (Rom. 8:28).

• ...that missionaries and supporters will understand that the greater the trials the greater the results for God's glory, both in heaven and on earth, and the greater the results for the kingdom in us and in the work (James 1:2, 5:11; 1 Peter 1:6,7).

CHAPTER 2
~ ~ Best Friend and Worst Enemy ~ ~

William Carey

Most interesting is William Carey's relationship with Dr. John Thomas. It doesn't seem that it could have been an accident that John came upon the scene at the time the Mission Society was being formed. With his experience and knowledge of Bengali, his zeal for evangelism, his medical profession and his willingness to be their first missionary, there seemed no question that this was part of God's plan. He even assured them that missionaries could support themselves on the field, which lightened the mission board's burden considerably.

William had not intended to be sent himself; it was John's information that there were scholars in India who were asking for help in translating the Bible that sparked the call for William to go. When he learned that John himself had done some translation and saw that his work was accurate, his heart leapt at the chance to go as the helper of such a person to answer the call for help in translation.

When the board heard of John Thomas's zeal for evangelism and saw his gifts for convincing people, they knew he was exactly the type of person they wanted to send. They did not neglect to check his story. One of them went to London to enquire about him and came back with very good reports. It seems amazing to me that the people they talked to either did not know of John's indebtedness or did not want to reveal it. If the board had known of it, most likely they would have refrained from sending him at that time. This too had to have been God's plan.

The sending board members had no idea that they should have been praying for Thomas's weaknesses; all they saw were his many strengths. Did any of them think to pray that John and William would be led "not into temptation and delivered from evil?" Did any pray for John that he would consider William's family's situation from the beginning as he spent the funds and made his plans? Or did they feel as we often do that his self-confident, pleasing personality and experience would automatically lead him to always do the right thing? I wonder if any read between the lines to pray as they looked at the situation.

There were very good reasons why William would consider John Thomas his best friend to the end. Without John's experience and efforts, it wasn't likely that William would have even been on the field.

On the sea voyage to India, the two confessed their sins and weaknesses to one another and must have prayed together, a very good exercise for people about to bring the light of the Gospel into a land that had been largely without it.

It was John who arranged for them to have positions managing indigo plantations and who sent the money for the Careys to leave the Sundarbans. He enabled the Careys to escape their despair in that place just before the monsoons arrived; the incessant rains would have increased their trials considerably. But of course, if John had paid attention to them in the beginning, they would not have ended up in that dreadful place.

It was John who came to help during their son, Peter's, illness. John and his wife were the ones who stood by William through Dolly's affliction, giving support and advice.

The man who had come to Christ earlier through John's witness, Ram Ram Basu, was a help to them in evangelism and translation work, though later he was caught in various types of sin and was let go.

It was John who led the first convert at Serampore to the Lord when he was called to set a broken shoulder for Krishna Pal, a Hindu carpenter. While treating Krishna, John explained the Gospel and helped him understand what it would cost him to follow Christ; he would lose his caste and probably be rejected by his family. But Krishna was ready to do that for Christ. He was baptized and served as a faithful evangelist and helper to his death. He was used to lead others to Christ, including some of his own family. "Sing, soul, sing," cried John at Krishna's conversion, "if it still can through my tears of fifteen years." It had been seven years since the Careys and the Thomases had arrived together before they saw this first fruit, and evidently John had labored eight years previously with no fruit (except Ram Ram Basu who did not last).

But there were also very good reasons why William could call John Thomas his "worst enemy." The fact that the doctor was running away from debts both in London and Calcutta could have brought disaster on the whole mission effort. In the providence of the Lord, it doesn't appear that it did, but we will never know how much harm was done. Fortunately, John did distance himself from the work when they established the mission in Serampore. William never knew all that John was doing or where he was much of the time.

It was primarily John who had convinced Dolly to go to India with them, telling her that she was doing an unwise thing by dividing the family and assuring her that she would always regret it if she did not go. The regrets turned out to be for William who wished later that they had followed their first agreement for her to stay in England with the younger children for a few years.

It was John who had told the mission board that missionaries could support themselves after getting to the field. This was a cause of hardship, especially for William and his family.

Had John paid enough attention to William's situation when they first arrived, he could have prevented their time in the Sundarbans, but he was too busy setting up his own family and practice in Calcutta and seemed to have forgotten about the Careys for a time.

On the day of Krishna's baptism, John suffered an episode of mental illness and had to be confined in the mission schoolhouse. Later, he stayed in a Calcutta asylum for a time. Biographer, George Smith, claims that John's "eccentric impulses and oft-darkened spirit were due to mania." Some believe he may have been, in today's terminology, manic-depressive.[9]

Nevertheless, William evidently was able to forgive and forget about the offenses and remember that John Thomas was his friend— his "best friend."

> In October (1801) Thomas died in Dingapore at the age of 45 from what they said was cholera. William reflected with great sadness, 'who could be sure?' All he knew was that India's many diseases relentlessly claimed missionaries: son Peter, Grant, John Fountain, David Brunsdon (three of the new missionaries who had arrived in 1799) and now John. John had been shunned and scorned and ridiculed his last years. But William had forgiven Him all of his idiosyncrasies long ago. Where would he be if he had not met exuberant, optimistic John Thomas? Where would

---

[9]   Vinita Hampton Wright, "Carey's Companions & Converts," *Christian History Magazine, Issue* 36, p. 33.

the Society be? Yes, John was flawed. But he had
a great heart. William would miss him deeply.[10]

Why is it that we expect our fellow workers and our missionaries to be perfect when we ourselves are not? Unfortunately, we all
still bear in our bodies the residue of the old sinful nature. Physical
ailments, mental deficiencies, or ailments and besetting sin all play
on our lives and actions. We can be helped by each other or by med-
icine, and we do have the promise that one day we will put off these
things when we go to be with Christ, but we never become perfect in
this life. Is that what Peter means in 1 Peter 4:8 when he writes, "And
above all things have fervent love for one another, for 'love will cover
a multitude of sins?'"

Our first years in Asia, 1964 to 1986, were spent at a children's
home. The parents of all of the children were suffering from Hanson's
disease. They were living on the streets or in leper colonies. The children were well when they came to the home at the ages of four or five,
but they were closely watched for the signs of the disease. In the early
stages, it could be treated without physical deformities resulting.

We had a friend who was a graduate of the home. He gave us
much advice and helped us to understand many things about his
community. But when in 1973 the board gave David the responsibility of opening an English medium school for the children of the
home, this friend became opposed to the idea. He felt that the children should not be taught in English. He considered that it would
take them out of their "culture," even though he put his own children
in a private English medium school to ensure their future prosperity.
Also, at that time, there was a nationalist movement emphasizing the
national language.

David and I and other fellow-workers felt that knowing and
becoming fluent in English would open doors for the children to
find a place in society where they would not be judged by their back-

---

[10] William Carey, *Father of Modern Missions by Sam Wellman*, (Uhrichsvillle, OH:
Barbour Publishing, Inc.), p. 164

grounds in the leper colonies but by their accomplishments. Even then, and more so now, any parents in that culture who could afford it would give their children English education. So, Home Academy was started.

This friend, however, managed to influence other key people at the home, and we found the work was being undermined. Eventually, we felt compelled to leave that situation. But an English school had been established, and for many years the children have studied in English and benefited. And though the school is not what it might have been academically, a wonderful work is being done in the lives of the children at the home. Many are believers. We consider that God knew exactly what they would need in the places where He would send them, in their own country or abroad, where many have gone.

And because we felt our job was therefore done at the home, God used David to meet a need at the theological seminary and then to develop a Christian English medium school in the same city that has a good reputation and is ministering to many students from Christian families, including the families of national missionaries and full-time Christian workers. It is attended by students from other religions in the neighborhood as well. Both of us were able to help in the planting of two churches in the city at the same time. It is one of our favorite examples of how God works all things together for good.

But perhaps the most upsetting case of betrayal by a "best friend" that we have seen happened again at the children's home after we had transferred and were still sitting on the board of the home. A large funding agency had come alongside the work in the 1970s when David was managing the home. The leaders of the organization were friends and Christians and appreciated our policies and goals for the children. They had previously invested some funds in an organization that had deceived them and were delighted to now find this work.

Through the ensuing years, this agency urged the home to take more and more children, all of whom were taken from the leper colonies. By 2005, the agency had helped the board to open three additional homes, and the number had gone up to eight hundred children in four homes.

But with their money, more and more strings were attached, and it seemed as if they came to feel that they owned the homes and should have the final word in directing the work, even though the institution was clearly under the responsibility of a local board registered under the government. While from the beginning support had been coming from several sources, those in charge relied more and more on the funds from this agency. A great work was done in those years, and many children were under the teaching of the Word and educated to lead productive lives.

By 2005, for various reasons, all of the board members and the CEO of this agency were changed and were now different people with new ideas. Though they had just a year before declared that this home was their finest work, showing the best results in the lives of children, they informed us that they were changing their policies. They now did not feel it wise to work with children in residential homes. The children should be with their parents at all costs, and the work they would fund was to be in the communities where the parents are living. They said we should change our policy to work with the children in the leper colonies and not bring them to homes. They would not hear our objection that we had children from around fifty colonies scattered far. It would be impossible to reach them all and give them quality teaching.

It was unthinkable that this work, which had been turning out young people of faith, to reach where we could never go, should stop. I grieved as though I were grieving for all who had already graduated and gone out until I realized the problem would not touch them. But oh to think that this wonderful ministry would not continue through future generations! Then I was comforted by one of the graduates over the phone, "Don't worry, Mom, it will be alright." And truly it did become so by the grace of the Lord and through the prayers and giving of many.

For a year, we argued with this organization, reminding them that the parents themselves, suffering from Hanson's disease, had begged us to take their children out of the colonies where they were at risk from not only disease but many forms of abuse. In the colonies, their chance of getting a good education was much less because of the prejudice against them as children of lepers. How could we possibly work with them while they lived with their parents?

But their ears were deaf to our pleas; their minds were set. When we told them it would be difficult for us to see the children come to faith and disciple them in the colonies, the CEO clearly said that didn't matter to them. You could almost say that our best friend had become our worst enemy, and a formidable enemy at that.

They had told us in 2006 that we were to take no new children into the homes. Our board decided to gently remind them that *it* was running the homes, not the donors, and took in twenty-six new children. To this day, I consider those children very specially "mine" because it was I who volunteered to raise sponsorships for new children from our friends and contacts in the United States and Australia. How we thank the Lord for people among our supporters who came forward and gave for their upkeep for many years and are still praying for those twenty-six children and the homes in general.

This made our former friends furious, and now they were determined to shut down the homes, and in the providence of the Lord, things got worse! A staff member at one of the new homes did not follow policies that should have been followed, resulting in an incident that broke our hearts. A girl was molested—by an outsider, not by a staff member. My husband, David, as president of the board, dealt with it properly as soon as it came to his knowledge. That staff member, who neglected to protect the girl, was immediately relieved of duty and spent some time in jail (though his offense was not the worst one but one of not following preventative guidelines). The guilty outsider was punished by the civil authorities. According to the parents' wishes, the home continued to look after the girl, educate her, and see her happily married. The staff member is still serving the Lord in another ministry, having learned, we trust, his lesson. But it was the final step in making our former friends our worst enemies.

Representatives of the agency demanded that the home board call a meeting for them, refused our hospitality, refused to hear any explanations of what really happened, and demanded that we all resign so that they could appoint their own board members. Undoubtedly, they would have appointed board members who would follow their wishes to close the homes. Later we learned that if we had all resigned from the board, it would not have been the agency that would have taken over but the government with which the board is registered. It would not have allowed such an illegal take-over, especially by a foreign body.

Of course, the threat of the organization was that they would immediately stop all funds if we did not cooperate. In the end, the home board refused to sign and was forced to accept that consequence. I will never forget the feeling of stepping out to trust the Lord for all of that money needed to maintain eight hundred children and the staff. Much prayer went up for money to pay the large bills every month.

The Lord proved faithful in answering and providing. Many churches and friends in the United States and Australia came forward. Our mission helped as much as possible. No children were turned out before their graduation from high school, but two of the smaller homes were closed, and those children were transferred to the other homes.

Our lawyer, who was of another faith, gave us comfort, "Trust the Lord," he said. "They cannot touch you." We went about our business, keenly aware that their representatives were running around all over the country, trying to find a lawyer who would take their case. We never heard anything more of it. The government was not going to allow any foreign body to interfere with an organization registered with them and doing such a commendable job with the children. Nor would they allow any foreign body to take back money or property they had given, which is what this agency thought it could do. The Lord answers the prayers of His people in interesting ways.

God had worked through the friendship of that organization to serve many children; we will always be grateful for that. Then, through the time when the same organization became an enemy, He worked to release the board from its enemy to continue to serve and care for children of future generations, keeping them under the hearing of the Word of God. Praise His name.

But that is not the end of the story. It gets better! When children were transferred from two of the homes where the educational facilities were not suitable, one of the properties was sold for a very good price to another Christian organization. That money was invested; interest on investments is very good. The income from that investment and others has made it possible for the home to be released from dependence on foreign funds. It tends to be always the goal of missionaries to see the institutions become financially independent. We never could have guessed how the Lord would answer prayer in that regard for these two homes. Praise His name.

Some national friends of ours built a house for their retirement in a neighborhood where most of their neighbors are Christians. Of course, they haven't really retired; their zeal and service hasn't slackened a bit since they moved there.

But their Christian friends next door have made things rather difficult for them. They tie their big dog at night outside of their house on the side toward our friends' bedroom window. The dog is very diligent about its watchdog duties. Its sharp bark rings out in the night, making it hard for our friends to get a good night's sleep.

We have given them the best ear plugs we can find, but that doesn't seem to be the solution. They have appealed to their neighbors, asking them to tie the dog on the other side of the house, but nothing changes. Each time we go to visit, we find them sleep-deprived and puzzled over what to do next.

Several drastic solutions have come to their minds, but they don't have the heart to apply them. They suffer on from the barking of the "Christian" dog next door. Their neighbors, previously friends, seem to have become enemies.

There are many issues that complicate relationships such as cultural matters, varying opinions on how to solve problems, unrealistic expectations of self and others, generational differences, suspicion, pride, jealousy, etc. It seems that all of the sins of human nature will be put to use by Satan to thwart God's work if the enemy is not properly resisted through prayer.

There was once a missionary friend of ours whose fellow missionary reported to the authority of the host government that he was involved in a plot to assassinate a high government official. The accusation was completely false of course, but it certainly disrupted that missionary's work and family for a time. The root of such an unthinkable act seemed to be jealousy on the part of the accuser, a fellow missionary. He had been stationed in a village area where he and his family experienced many inconveniences while the accused was stationed in the city. Where were the prayer warriors that the enemy gained such an apparent victory?

PRAY...

- ...that the work of Satan and his emissaries will be thwarted in the lives and ministries of those you are holding up. The promise is "Draw near to God, *resist* the Devil, and he will flee from you" (James 4:7).
- ...that your missionaries, aware of their own weaknesses, will have the grace to work with the weaknesses and different points of view of their fellow workers, whether missionaries or nationals.
- ...that they will know when to go their separate ways in the face of ongoing lack of unity among coworkers.
- ...that the Lord will give them the faith to believe through it all that truly for those who are serving the Lord, all things work together for good as promised in Romans 8:28.
- ...that they may be enabled to always return good for evil, or what seems like evil to them.
- ...that they, both missionaries and nationals, will have the Spirit of Christ who will help them love fervently, forgive their fellow workers, and set an example of following Christ.

CHAPTER 3
~ ~ *Living by Faith* ~ ~

Lillian Trasher

It was 1904. Lillian Trasher, age seventeen, was leaving her home in Asheville, North Carolina, to go to Atlanta, Georgia, and apply for a job as an artist with a newspaper. Her older sister, Jennie, nine years older than Lillian, had already left home to work as a stenographer in Long Beach, California

Lillian happened to pick a seat on the train beside Mattie Perry who was running an orphanage of a hundred children in Marion, North Carolina. During the journey, Mattie, sensing that Lillian was a Christian, invited her to become her assistant at the orphanage, telling her that she didn't believe anything happened by chance. "I think that we were meant to sit together and that I was meant to tell you about the orphanage." Lillian thought that was very amusing but told her she would think about it. Mattie left her with the words, "There is no end to what you can do if you follow God's call and trust Him to take care of the rest."

On the way to Atlanta, Lillian stopped in the neighborhood where her family had lived before they went to Asheville. There she visited the friend whose family had taken her to church and led her to the Lord. She rededicated her life to serve the Lord. "Lord," she said, "if ever I can do anything for You, just let me know, and—and I'll do it."

During her first few days in Atlanta, there was a misunderstanding at the newspaper office. The first person who interviewed Lillian led her to believe she had a very good chance of getting the job, but the next time she went back, she was told that an excellent person had already been hired. She went home and cried herself to sleep. When she woke up, she was no longer distressed. She knew that God was leading her to work in the orphanage in North Carolina.

When she returned to the newspaper office later to pick up the sketches she had left on her first visit, she found that she herself had been the "excellent person" who had been chosen. But since she didn't show up for work, they had hired someone else. She responded with a smile, "I have a wonderful life ahead of me. Thank you for everything."[11]

For the next five years, Lillian's life was full. She learned the hard life of caring for children and living on very little money without a regular income. She also experienced the joy of "preaching around the South" with some of Mattie's relatives and attended a local Bible college.

On one of her trips, she met a fine young preacher named Tom. They fell in love and were planning to marry. But ten days before the wedding, Lillian accompanied Mattie to hear a missionary from

---

[11] Janet Benge and Geoff Benge, *Lillian Trasher: the Greatest Wonder in Egypt* (Seattle: YWAM Pub., 2004), L119-275

India speak. As he spoke, tears began streaming down her face. That night, she did not sleep as she realized that God was calling her to be a missionary, and she felt the call was to Africa.

She knew this meant that she could not marry Tom as he did not have a call to Africa, and this caused many tears. Tom offered to wait a few years for her, but Lillian somehow knew that she was meant to spend her whole life in a foreign place and never live in the United States again.[12]

History testifies to the fact that God has called many, many single women to serve Him at home and around the world. Paul makes it clear in 1 Corinthians 7:34b and 35 that single women and men are better able to devote themselves to the Lord. Many have proved that true and done wonderful things for the Lord at home and abroad. And Lillian is a very good example.

A week later, Lillian heard about a holiness missionary conference to be held in Pittsburgh, Pennsylvania, and felt that was where she should go. Friends gave her money to make the trip, but it was enough to get her only to Washington, DC. She felt she should go there and wait for the money to complete the trip. Mattie gave her the name of friends with whom she could stay in the city. "She left with one small bag, a dollar in her purse, and the burning desire to be a missionary. Lillian's church in Asheville, the Buxton Street Holiness Church, could not support her financially, and her parents were set against the idea of her new career."[13]

At the home where she was a guest that night in Washington, DC, there happened to be three missionaries from Egypt who were also guests. She told Rev. Brelsford, one of the missionaries, that she was called to be a missionary to Africa. He was quite amazed that she had no mission board, no support except for one dollar in her pocket, no help from her parents, and didn't know where in Africa she was to go. Rev. Brelsford told her she should go right back to her parents. She would have been about twenty-two at this point.

---

[12] Ibid, L 293-341
[13] Ibid, L 358

Lillian carefully avoided the subject of her call again until the second day of her stay when Rev. Brelsford said to her, "After discussing things with my wife, and after praying about it, I must confess I was hasty in what I said yesterday. Can you forgive me for doubting your call?—We are used to doing things in an orderly manner, and it just seemed preposterous to us. However, God does work in mysterious ways and we can see that you have faith—that is the key. My wife and I run a mission home in Assiout (Sometimes spelled Asyut), Egypt. I am not in a position to offer you money of any kind, but if you find your way to Assiout, we could provide your meals and lodging and you could work with us."

It wasn't long before Lillian knew that this was the next step for her. She was on her way to being a missionary in Africa.

Funds to travel to Pittsburgh for the conference and back to New York came from somebody who owed her money. But after the conference, when she and Mr. Brelsford, who was going on a tour before returning to Egypt, got to the ticket office, he found that he did not have quite enough money for his ticket. Lillian made up his shortfall, and after counting what she had left, discovered she had only enough to get to Harrisburg. A friend had sent her the address of a Christian couple in Harrisburg where she found hospitality for the night.

When she was taken to the station to leave again, her host asked her if she had the money for her ticket. The man was shocked to find she had no money and gave her the amount for her fare to New York. He asked how she expected to get all the way to Egypt. "If God wants me there, God will get me there. I believe He is looking after that need right now."

In New York, she stayed at the Glad Tidings Mission for a time. She spoke at the mission on Sunday and soon was invited to speak at various mission meetings and churches around the city. A collection was taken up, and by the end of August, she had saved forty dollars, which she put down at the travel office on her passage. Then she informed her parents and her sister, Jennie, that she was sailing for Africa on the eighth of October.

Surprising news came from her sister, Jennie. She was going to go with her in case she needed help along the way, but she intended to stay only until Lillian was settled.

The day before Jennie arrived, Lillian was feeling sick with anxiety. She dreaded telling Jennie that she didn't have the rest of the money for her ticket. A loud knock was heard on the door of the mission. Being the only one at home, Lillian answered to find a woman asking for her. The woman enquired about her plans, knelt in front of her, and prayed, thanking the Lord for providing all of Lillian's needs and handed her $60 before leaving. When Lillian rushed to the door to see which direction she had gone, she had already melted into the crowd. Lillian wrote in her diary that night, "My God shall supply all your needs."

When Lillian and Jennie arrived in Assiout on November 10, 1910, they were amazed to find a beautiful city by the Nile. The land around the city was lush, green, and dotted with palm trees. She learned that the city had been home to Coptic Christians for centuries. The Coptic Church claims St. Mark as its founder. Many of the people in the area were Christians.[14]

Things went well. Jennie, though she didn't like the cold weather of Egypt in the winter season, did not make preparations to leave.

One evening, about three months after their arrival, there came a knock at the door. Lillian had a feeling that day that something significant was going to happen. A man was asking for someone to go and help a young mother who was dying. Somehow Lillian knew that the man had come for her, and she persuaded Rev. Brelsford to let her go. An older woman missionary and their handyman accompanied her. The three of them returned with an emaciated baby girl. The young mother's dying words had been, "Please take her," and the man who had come to the door had disappeared. The only other person on the scene was a great grandmother who indicated the child should be thrown into the river.

---

[14] Janet Benge and Geoff Benge, *Lillian Trasher: the Greatest Wonder in Egypt* (Seattle: YWAM Pub., 2004), L365-527

Lillian had clung to the baby and headed for the mission house saying, "I will find a way to care for you. Surely the Rev. and Mrs. Brelsford will let me take in a desperate little one like you."[15]

Lillian and Jennie were allowed to keep the baby and care for it at the mission house. But it was so sickly that for many nights it kept everyone in the house awake with its wailing. Finally, after two weeks with no change, Rev. Brelsford told Lillian to take the baby back. Knowing full well that there was no place to take her where she would be cared for, Lillian would not part with the baby. She agreed to take the baby away, saying, "But I will go with her."

This shocked Mr. Brelsford who felt responsible for her welfare. He warned her that it would not be safe for her to live alone in Egypt. "A lone American woman living in an Arabic world? You will be killed, or you'll starve to death."

She retorted, "I won't be alone. I will have God with me."

His response was, "If you leave this house with the baby, you leave without my permission—but if things go wrong, don't come back here begging for help." I wonder if he ever regretted that statement.

What Mr. Brelsford perhaps didn't realize is that a woman looking after children is generally looked upon favorably in such cultures more than a woman by herself. In Asia, I felt much safer when I had children with me than when I was completely alone. People have a great deal of sympathy for children and especially orphans.

Jennie, of course, did not allow her to go alone. That very day, she and Jennie found a house to rent in the city. After buying the bare necessities for the house, they had only enough money left to eat until the end of the month.

Thus began a lifetime for Lillian of finding ways to care for and educate orphans and widows "by faith." For fifty-one years, she took in children and widows, built buildings, and raised money among the Egyptian people, tourists, the Assemblies of God churches in the United States, and any other sources she could find. She endured privations and dangers of plague, war, uprisings, and persecution to care

---

[15] Ibid. L527-570

for a total that, over her fifty-one years of ministry, was estimated at around ten thousand souls.[16] Lillian's story will be continued in the next chapter.

Working by faith means different things to different people. To some it means not having a mission board or any other authority but God to report to and not having anybody but God to give advice or tell them what to do. They rarely listen to advice and believe that if they follow their own inclinations or dreams, they are "living by faith." That description is an oversimplification perhaps, but often some degree of that attitude is implied when people say they are "faith missionaries."

To others, it means they don't have any regular source of income. Sometimes, they won't even tell anybody else about the needs for the work but insist that God has to deal with those who are to supply the need Himself. Wonderful people have felt led to work that way, George Mueller being one of the best examples. I don't know whether Lillian would have used the term, "faith missionary," to describe herself. I think following God by faith and depending on Him through prayer just came naturally to her. She did make her needs known in her local area and in the United States, as well as among the tourists who would stop in Assiout on their way down the Nile.

At one school where we worked, when national workers came for admission, the term, "faith missionary," was sometimes used to let us know they would not be able to pay even the subsidized fees that the school charges national workers. The school authorities were expected to have the faith that produced the costs.

One interesting note here is the fact that work with orphans or similarly disadvantaged children has more of an appeal for people to give money than other ministries do. Other missionaries would occasionally remind us of how much easier our job was when we represented the Children's Home than theirs when they were raising

---

[16] Janet Benge and Geoff Benge, *Lillian Trasher: the Greatest Wonder in Egypt* (Seattle: YWAM Pub., 2004), L1834

it for other ministries. Did that mean they had to have more faith? Perhaps.

I would certainly not criticize any of these people. My goal is to help us understand missions today and suggest how we should be praying. We, too, must know how to live and work "by faith." The Word says, "The just shall live by faith" (Rom. 1:16). What does that really mean for us and for our missionaries?

Perhaps we could define living by faith or being faith missionaries as trusting Christ for our salvation and ability and provision to serve Him, obeying Him in all that is revealed in His Word, looking to Jesus for the next step as we follow Him, and trusting Him to provide through whatever means He chooses, regular and predictable or otherwise.

Issues like this as they work with people of differing views will at some time or another face your missionaries, and they will have to work them through. Your *prayers* can help as they do.

As we shall read in the next chapter, even Lillian became so weak and discouraged during the privations of the Great Depression that she was ready to send the children away. It was the prayers of the children that saved her from such a step, and God answered them in an amazing way. We must pray for our missionaries that their faith will not fail in the difficult times they will surely face.

We found ourselves, after finishing our education, with much to learn about the life of faith. We had committed our lives to do His will, hoping and praying it would take us to service in the land of David's birth in Asia. Truly our prayers were answered. We were approached by a sister denomination of the one to which we belonged. Their missions committee was looking for replacements for a missionary couple who had, in their later years of ministry, started a children's home. In the providence of the Lord, we would be able to get "replacement visas" since the missionaries who had established the home were leaving the country to retire in the United States.

Our faith felt very rewarded and strong at that point. When we sailed for the field six months later, we had no idea how much we would need the prayers of the people in our sending churches as well as of our supportive family and friends that our faith would not fail.

The money that came regularly for our salary was sufficient for the simple standard of living that was appropriate at the children's home, living with other missionaries at first and then establishing our own home in one of the staff residences at the institution. But we soon realized that adequate funds were not coming to properly care for the 135 or so children in the home.

We were pleased on our first furlough, after five years on the field, that the small denomination we had gone out with had united with a larger one that had its own mission board. That board required its missionaries to raise their support. As we did, visiting churches and individuals, we were able to raise support for the children's home as well as for our support account at the mission from individuals and churches. And later we did the same as we helped establish two other institutions.

This matter of how to raise money for missions can be a hindrance sometimes for your missionaries. Some people, though called to missions, can find it awkward to go from place to place, presenting the need for support. They feel as though they are begging. And sometimes it is a rather humbling experience. But we always reminded ourselves that we were simply giving others an opportunity to have a part in this exciting work of the kingdom. We did not press people to give but merely told of the wonderful things the Lord was doing and offered people the chance to have a part in God's work by giving and/or praying. We felt as though God would call those who would take advantage of the opportunity.

More faith was required of us twenty-five-year-old missionaries to make a decision on a policy issue with which we were soon confronted. A senior (in her seventies) missionary had as her role model Lillian Trasher. I honestly did not realize that until after I did research on Lillian for this book. This dear woman of faith with whom we were working believed as Lillian did, that as many children who came should be taken in.

This issue comes back to the question missionaries often face. Are they going to help a lot of people a little, or are they going to help a limited number as much as they need to be helped? It is faced and grappled with in many areas of life, in politics, in mission committee meetings, in your churches, etc. When it comes to raising children, the question needs to be settled fairly early because every child you take in involves a commitment for many years.

David and I, and one other young missionary couple, who were working at the home at the time, came down on the side of helping a limited number as much as possible. We were already committed to raising and educating those 135 children; and their diet, living conditions, and education needed considerable improvement. The issue came to a head when at the annual one-day meeting of the parents with their children, arranged at a location about a two-hour drive from the home, a surprising event took place.

A limited number of new children had been admitted, and the buses had been loaded for all of the children to return to the home. As they pulled away, parents somehow pushed about twenty-five more children onto the buses through the windows. Of course, that pointed to the problems of not adequate staff and proper supervision, which was another issue we felt needed to be addressed before taking many more children.

When the buses arrived at the home and the stowaway children were discovered, we younger missionaries insisted that they must be returned, thinking that parents should learn that they must deal with us in an orderly fashion. It would have been difficult, but we had people who knew the leaders and parents in the colonies well enough that they could have traced them back to their parents.

But the lady who thought like Lillian Trasher, that no child should ever be turned away, insisted that they must stay. The end of the discussion was that she took the extra children and started another home. Soon after that, the other young missionary couple went to a new location and eventually started another home where the number was to be kept to forty and be boys only. All three homes are still in existence today.

Now that required some faith to walk through that situation in our first few years on the field; we had to remember how clearly God had given us the assurance that He had complete control of the circumstances. As William Carey prayed, when he felt guilt about his bumbling efforts and his difficulty with his wife, "When I reflect, Lord, how You stirred me up into this work and how You prepared my way, then I can trust Your promises and be at peace that this work is part of Your plan."[17]

Now, in my old age, I find myself perhaps more on the side of quantity than quality. Thankfully, improving the quality of care and education at the homes has been and is still being addressed as well as possible, and the standard of living of the children and their education is much better than it was in 1965. But from my vantagepoint now, I tend to think that keeping as many children (or people in general) as possible under the hearing of the Word of God is perhaps more important than raising standards of living. Keeping the balance between quantity and quality is a life-long struggle, and we would do well to pray for our missionaries as they face it in their work.

PRAY...

- ...that the faith of your missionaries will remain strong.
- ...that they will learn more and more how to trust the Lord and walk by faith.
- ...that they will remember their call when problems and doubts come.
- ...that they will enjoy the important part of their ministry that takes place away from their field of service: visiting and reporting to supporters and raising prayer and financial support; offering people the opportunity to have a part in what God is doing.
- ...that their support and the resources needed for their special projects will come quickly.
- ...that they will have a good balance between quantity and quality in their work.

---

[17] William Carey, *Father and Modern Missions, by Sam Wellman.* (Uhrichsvillle, OH: Barbour Publishing, Inc.), p. 112

CHAPTER 4
~ ~ Enduring by Faith ~ ~

Lillian reading to her sister, Jennie

Lillian Trasher was the featured missionary in the previous chapter. We noted the faith that caused her to follow the Lord step by step to becoming a missionary in Egypt. In this chapter, we will continue her story.

As was explained in the last chapter, early in 1911, Mr. Brelsford had told Lillian and her sister, Jennie, that they could not raise children at the mission house in Assiout, Egypt. They had already accepted their first abandoned baby, whom they had named Fareida, so they rented another house. From that time on, the local people began to help them. They would leave money or food at the doorstep.

Lillian would ride on a donkey into the villages to visit people and almost always come back with money and supplies for the children.

Several more children were added to the number, and later in 1911, they welcomed a homeless boy named Habib to their household, making it a total of four children. The day after his arrival, Habib came down with bubonic plague. Soon, Lillian herself was suffering from plague. Both survived, but the doctor insisted Lillian would ruin her heart if she did not rest long enough to completely recover. She was not inclined to rest, but the neighbors promised to take turns helping Jenny with the children if she would go away to rest. They kept their promises while Lillian and the baby, Fareida, went to Alexandria to rest, using money their neighborhood friends had raised.

By 1914, their household numbered eight children whom they were schooling as well as caring for. They felt the need of more space. With wonderful provision through local people and the labor of the older boys making their own bricks, a proper orphanage was erected on their own land across the Nile. By Christmas 1916, they were able to move into their own building.

While the building was going up, Lillian came back to the house one day to find a man watching the children. He looked familiar. Suddenly her heart sank. She remembered that he was the man who had come to the mission house to find someone to care for the baby, Fareida, now four years old. She quickly gathered her into her arms but to no avail. The man had an official paper giving him the right to the child.

Fareida cried as he took her away and Lillian cried for many nights. "She did not think she could be any more heartbroken until she received the news that Fareida had died. The little girl had been happy and in perfect health when her father took her away."[18]

In 1917, the Great War was taking a terrible toll on the people of Egypt. The British were taking more and more of the men to fight, leaving women and children destitute. Many orphans were taken into the orphanage. One mother with four children, starving, came

---

[18] Janet Benge and Geoff Benge, *Lillian Trasher: the Greatest Wonder in Egypt* (Seattle: YWAM Pub., 2004), L764-970

to the gate and asked for all five of them to be taken in. Lillian could not bear to tell the woman they were taking only children. "Are you prepared to work?" she asked her. "I would do anything to stay with my children," was her tearful reply.[19] So began the policy of taking in widows, as well as children, which proved an asset to Lillian as the widows shared in the task of caring for the little ones.

On New Year's Day 1918, there were fifty orphans and eight widows in their care. The orphanage was running smoothly, and Lillian felt it was time to write a formal policy for running the home. Three of the eleven points were

1. "There shall be no limit to the number of orphans accepted."
2. "Relatives must sign a paper that they give the children to us until they are eighteen years old."
3. "The orphanage shall not only clothe and feed its family but give religious training and education and teach the trades of the land to each orphan as required."

In November 1918, Jenny returned to her home in California. She had stayed by Lillian's side over seven more years than originally planned.

The war ended in November 14, 1918, but it did not bring peace to Egypt. The British had taken over the country in order to protect the Suez Canal, but after the war, they did not leave. Their harsh rule brought on a rebellion that brought danger to Lillian as a foreigner and to the orphanage. It would not be the first time in history that American missionaries suffered in reprisals against the British, as we shall see.

The night the rebels arrived in the town of Assiout near the orphanage she led the children (107 by that time) to a kiln on the property where thick brick walls would protect them from the bullets. But after arriving, she counted and discovered that two toddlers were missing. Risking her life, she ran to the orphanage and found them. Carrying one under each arm, she ran back, narrowly escaping

---

[19]   Ibid, L990

two men intent on killing anyone who looked British. As a bullet whizzed past her head, she fell, rolled into a ditch, and struggled to keep the children quiet. She could hear the men talking about how much they wanted to kill this English woman. One of the children whimpered, and the men grew silent. Suddenly, a loud voice called them away and they retreated.[20]

The next morning, she found the orphanage had not been plundered or destroyed except for some bullet holes in the walls. Thinking the marauders had all left, she took the children back. But that evening, a group broke through the door and threatened to kill her until a neighbor (the only one that hadn't fled from his near-by decimated farm), named Said, came and stood in front of her, saying to them, "This woman has taken in our Egyptian orphans and widows. She has given herself to serve them. She has done us nothing but good."[21] After some very tense moments, while Said stood firm and stared down the would-be murderers, with Lillian praying silently, the gang turned and stomped out. She had narrowly escaped death twice within twenty-four hours.

A few days later, a group of British soldiers came marching and knocked on her door. She was very glad to see them until they gave her the news that all foreigners had been ordered to leave and take refuge in Cairo. How could she leave her children? But the soldiers had their orders and go with them she must. She took some of the children with her to the nearby city for the night, intending to plead her case with the general in the morning.

As soon as they passed the gate, the sobbing started and continued until they were settled at the Presbyterian hospital for the night, and the children fell asleep from exhaustion. Lillian continued miserable until about 3:00 a.m. when a calm came over her. Her mind was at rest for the first time in days. She prayed, "Lord, is there something You want to say to me?" Then the idea came that instead of going to Cairo, she should go back to the States to raise money

[20] Janet Benge and Geoff Benge, *Lillian Trasher: the Greatest Wonder in Egypt* (Seattle: YWAM Pub., 2004), L1043-1088
[21] Ibid, 1120

for the work and encourage people to pray.[22] She recognized it as the leading of God.

Kissing each child and promising she would be back, she left Egypt with the same brown bag (suitcase), containing only a change of clothes and pen and paper, that she had come with nine years before.

In California, with Jenny and her mother who was now living with Jenny, she became acquainted with the Assemblies of God Church. She felt at home with them and joined. Then she went on a nationwide tour that included a good number of Assemblies of God churches and raised much financial and prayer support for the orphanage. Lillian considered that prayer was just as important as material goods and money. She was able to send money back for the orphanage and put a good sum into a bank account.

By the spring of 1920, it was safe for "Mother Trasher," as she was known all over Egypt by now, to return, and she found that those left in charge had done a good job. More children had been taken, and there was need for another dormitory. It was at this time that she began raising money from tourists sailing down the Nile. She went onto the boats when they docked at the nearby city, passing out leaflets, describing the orphanage, and inviting people to visit. Much money was raised this way.

By 1924, there were three hundred children in the orphanage. About this time some wealthy Egyptian women bought her a car as they didn't like to see her riding around on a donkey.

On April 7, 1927, Lillian described a revival that came upon the community. At devotions one night, April 7, 1927, Lillian had read a passage from the Bible when:

> She became aware of sniffles and sobs around the room. Suddenly children began to get down on their knees and confess their sins aloud to God and ask Him to forgive them and make them new people inside. Soon the sound of prayer and

---

[22] Ibid, 1166

confession drowned out Lillian. The meeting went on long into the night, and when the children were sent to bed, they continued to pray in groups in their dormitory rooms or alone lying on their beds.[23]

The next day, the children asked to go into the city and share what had happened, and many people became Christians. The pattern went on for five days. and many lives were turned around. A renewed sense of love spread through the orphanage. Lillian was delighted, for that is the ultimate goal of any missionary, to see lives changed by the work of the Holy Spirit in the name of Jesus Christ.

But the valley ahead after this mountain top was truly deep. The great depression engulfed the world. In 1927, the annual income at the orphanage was nearly twenty-five thousand dollars. By 1933, it had plummeted to under fifteen thousand. But far worse for Lillian was when the tide of public opinion turned against Christians looking after Muslim children, and the government took from her orphanage seventy children who were from Muslim families and put them in a Muslim institution.

The numbers had risen by then to 700 but dropped to 650 by the end of 1933. Lillian was in one way happy to not have so many mouths to feed. She was mentally and physically exhausted. Her blood pressure was high, and after a two-month bout of illness, she did not feel she could go on. Feeling that she no longer had the strength to trust God for help, she called the community together and told them they would all have to go home or to friends, knowing full well many had neither. Their response was what she herself had taught them and demonstrated from the beginning. They fell to their knees and earnestly prayed that they would not have to leave. She followed their example and fell to her knees. After several minutes, a calm came over her. "I cannot send you away," she said. "If we do without, we will do without together. We all need to keep praying." And that night, each

---

[23] Ibid, 1335

had a bit of rice cooked in a lot of water and a quarter piece of bread for supper. When they urged Lillian to eat her share, she would not.

The next day, they had no food or money. By lunch time, there was still nothing. Lillian sent for the mail, and opening the last letter, she found a check for one thousand dollars. The children cheered. Lillian looked at the envelope. It had been addressed to Lillian Trasher, Assiout, *India!* How had it reached them in their hour of need in Egypt? She guessed that someone in the post office in Kansas must have known she lived in Egypt and routed it properly.

The $1,000 was enough for supplies for three days or maybe five if it were carefully stretched. But from that time, the money began to flow in again. Lillian wrote to her supporters in the States, "How I love my work and thank God that he chose me and not someone else, but I am so tired…"[24]

On September 27, 1937, Lillian celebrated her fiftieth birthday. By then, there were over seven hundred children. In 1939, an article came out in the *Reader's Digest* titled, "Nile Mother." As a result of this, much more money came in.

And then came World War II. The orphanage now contained nine hundred children. All of the people of Egypt were suffering. The children were down to half a cup of lentils each for dinner. Their clothes were in tatters. One evening, she announced that schoolwork would be suspended for twenty-four hours so that everyone could pray in earnest. They prayed all day until 2:30 a.m., and Lillian and staff continued after that.

In the morning, a telegram arrived from the American ambassador to Egypt in Cairo. She was to meet him the next day for lunch. A Red Cross cargo ship had been turned back from Greece, which had fallen to the Germans. It was in port at Alexandria. The captain had been ordered to dump the supplies and head out to sea under cover of darkness. A Scottish sailor knew of the orphanage and had begged the captain to unload the supplies in port instead of dumping them

---

[24] Janet Benge and Geoff Benge, *Lillian Trasher: the Greatest Wonder in Egypt* (Seattle: YWAM Pub., 2004), L1507

at sea. The captain argued that they didn't have time, but the sailor insisted there was time, and the ship had been unloaded.

"Tell me, Miss Trasher, do you have a need for food and clothing at this time?"

Lillian let out a gasp. "What did you say?" she asked.

The Ambassador smiled and said he would arrange for the cost of transporting the supplies to the orphanage. There was much rejoicing at the orphanage upon her return at the wonderful way God had answered their prayers. No sooner had she arrived back home when truckloads of supplies began pouring through the gate and the children eagerly helped to unload them. By the end of the war, most of the children were still wearing clothes from the *Kassandra Louloudis*.[25]

Things brightened up after the war until September 1947, when another horror came to Egypt in the form of cholera. People died by the thousands. Death came within hours of the victim's realizing he had the disease. All schools were closed except Lillian's, since those children were together all the time anyhow. Lilliam dreaded to think what would happen if one child contracted the disease. It would spread like wildfire.

Closer and closer the disease came to Assiout. People were told to have as little contact with others as possible, but the orphanage had a constant stream of visitors, deliverymen, and helpers. Lillian thought she should not take in any new children during the epidemic, but she couldn't stand the thought of doing what had never been done; turning away a needy child.

Finally, the disease reached Assiout. She saw the white circle on a house as she returned from the city. It was not long after that when a knock came at the door one morning. There stood a father with two young boys, Musa and Ibrahim, whose mother had died. He had walked four days to get there, and he wanted to leave them. She told the person who brought the message that they could not take new children during the epidemic. But before the message reached the gate, Lillian, unable to turn them away, had herself arrived at the

---

[25] Ibid, 1623

gate to greet them and take them in. How she prayed that she had done the right thing.

The two new boys spent the day running around with the other children. Around midnight, Lillian was awakened with the news that one of them had 105 temperature and the symptoms of cholera. Her worst nightmare had come true! Musa was taken to an isolation ward at the hospital and died within hours. The health department came, and they all worked together at disinfecting the dormitory. Ibrahim was kept in isolation. But God had mercy and not one other person was infected. In another six months, the cholera epidemic subsided in Egypt.

The following years brought great expansion for the orphanage. A small hospital was built. A man from Philadelphia donated enough money to erect a church that seated one thousand people. New dormitories were added along with a bigger barn to house the twenty-five milking cows. And there was a huge swimming pool donated by a wealthy Egyptian.

In 1953, the prime minister of Egypt came to visit and was greatly impressed. He declared an annual "Lillian Trasher Day," when local merchants were encouraged to make donations to the orphanage.

When she would visit Cairo, Lillian would be entertained by her grown children and their children. There were little boys named Trasher and girls named Lillian all over Egypt. Whichever house she would stay in, others would gather. Many had done very well in their occupations; this, of course, gave her much joy.

A biography of her life was written and a documentary film made titled *The Nile Mother*. This brought many more donations and more expansion. This documentary film, featuring Lillian Trasher in her last years, can still be seen on the web.

Around 1956, her sister, Jennie, who had visited Egypt from time to time, sold her property in California and returned permanently to work alongside Lillian. The two of them had started the orphanage together, and now they would grow old together serving in it.

In 1960, Lillian made another visit to the States to speak at a series of Assemblies of God Sunday School conventions. She challenged people to make a start on what they felt God had told them to do and not to wait for all the pieces to fall into place first. "Once you know it's God's will," she said, "get moving! At the orphanage, we start a new building project as soon as we have three bricks to put on top of each other."[26]

When she visited Houston, she was shown to a fancy hotel room in the heart of Houston. But when she read the sign on the door that said it was costing $18 a night, she phoned her host and declared, "That money would buy the milk my children would need at the orphanage. I am sorry, but I can't spend one night in a bed that costs as much as the milk for my babies would cost." She spent the rest of her time in the US staying in Christian homes. No one made the mistake of booking her into a hotel again.[27]

Near the end of her visit, Lillian began having dizzy spells, which a doctor confirmed were related to her high blood pressure. She cut short the last week of her visit to return home. For several weeks after returning, her life hung in the balance.

Finally, on Sunday, December 17, 1961, a day when two new babies were welcomed into the orphanage, Lillian Trasher died at the age of seventy-four. Jennie was at her side. Lillian had been in the Assiout hospital for ten weeks with heart problems.

A horse-drawn carriage carried Lillian's body slowly through the streets of Assiout back to the orphanage. Both Christians and Muslims wept as Mama Lillian's casket passed. Approximately 1200 stunned children lined up in silence as they tried to grasp what had happened. A solemn ceremony was held in the huge orphanage church. Her body was buried in the orphanage cemetery, surrounded by the graves of several of the children.[28] And so ended an amazing journey of faith.

---

[26] Janet Benge and Geoff Benge, *Lillian Trasher: the Greatest Wonder in Egypt* (Seattle: YWAM Pub., 2004), L1788

[27] Ibid, 1806

[28] Janet Benge and Geoff Benge, *Lillian Trasher: the Greatest Wonder in Egypt* (Seattle: YWAM Pub., 2004), L1833

Let us read "between the lines" a bit by looking closely, not at Lillian but at Jennie. Here was a woman who saw the need of her younger sister and went to a great deal of sacrifice to meet it. She knew a young girl should not be going off by herself to a strange land.

Little did she know that the seeming impetuosity of her sister would keep her in Egypt for over seven years (impetuosity sometimes appears to accompany faith).

It seems that Jennie had not been consulted when Lillian clasped Fareida in her arms and headed home, though probably Jennie too saw that it was the only thing to do. Jennie did not know when Lillian went off to rent a house with the baby. The first Jennie knew of it was when the house had already been rented and Lillian was packing. Note is made in the biography that Lillian herself realized how unfair that was to Jennie. But still Jennie didn't let her go alone to take in more children, face deprivation, and survive a major illness. She stuck with her through World War I and the influx of orphans and widows created at that time. Perhaps because Lillian had started taking in mothers with the children, Jennie felt there was then enough help that she herself could go home and give her attentions to looking after her property in California and taking care of their parents.

We know of Jennie because she was mentioned in Lillian's biography, but it has been our experience that there are hundreds of such people who contribute to the work of people who become well-known, both on the field and at home. And it is hard for the well-known person to give ample credit to all who deserve it, no matter how much they may want to do so. God knows, and that is really what matters. But my point is that we should pray for such people who surround our missionaries, even though we often don't know their names.

In our later years, we thought it helpful to let the people in the churches know the extent of the work of our mission when we spoke in churches. It was my job to give that overview. But becoming aware that it tended to make people think more highly of us than we deserved, I started adding, "Now don't think that we did this all single-handedly. There were many other nationals and missionaries involved in this work. It is a description of *God's* work as He built His kingdom in that part of the world. We just have the privilege of telling you about it."

PRAY…

- …that your missionaries will have the faith to endure whatever trials God sends.
- …that they will be aware of the power of the Holy Spirit working in and through them.
- …that those to whom the missionaries are ministering will be able to hold them up in prayer at times when their faith and strength may falter, as the children prayed for Lillian in her time of weakness.
- …that your missionaries will appreciate those upon whom they depend in the Lord's work, will regularly pray for them and encourage their supporters to do so as well.
- …that the Lord will send capable, prayerful, faithful workers, both missionaries and nationals, to work alongside your missionaries.
- …that your missionaries will not think more highly of themselves than they should or allow others to do so.

CHAPTER 5
~ ~ Betrayal and Deceit ~ ~

Slaughter of Missionaries in Indian Mutiny of 1857

Some of the missionaries you know may face worse than a "best friend, worst enemy" relationship. Some may be deliberately betrayed, resulting in harm to themselves and the work.

Albert O. and Amanda Gill Johnson went to India as Presbyterian missionaries in 1855, arriving with four other new missionaries. The mission of the Presbyterian Church in the USA at that time was much like the PCA in its evangelistic zeal; the Lord's work was flourishing in northwest India.

At a gathering in December of 1855, Presbyterian missionaries from a number of stations united into what they named the

Furrukhabad Mission. The meetings lasted ten days and the occasion was recorded as a "very delightful one."[29]

But according to the records:

> The year 1857 opened auspiciously, and no one of the busy and hopeful mission band dreamed how darkly it would close. The schools were very prosperous, the press was doing a noble work, translation work was being vigorously prosecuted—and there seemed unwonted interest in the Gospel message.
>
> But the letters sent to America in May carried the startling tidings of the mutiny among the (Indian) troops in Meerut, and of the increasing disaffection in the native regiments in other cities in North India. On June 2nd, Mr. McMullin wrote of the "danger now so imminent" and on June 3rd, Mr. Ullmann wrote from Agra that he and his family "fled for their lives."
>
> The missionaries in Agra, together with the children boarding in the schools, took refuge in the fort. From the ramparts, Mr. Fullerton saw the first torch of the incendiary applied to the buildings occupied by Europeans. The normal school for the education of native teachers was first fired; and, in a short time, five miles of the station were in flames.
>
> People continued to flock into the fort for protection, until Mr. Scott wrote, 'We have a resident population of 6,000, and many more during the day." Here the wounded were brought, and the missionaries were able to render much valuable aid in caring for the suffering.

---

[29] *India Missions: Historical Sketches* (Allahabad, U.P. India: Allahabad Mission Press), pp. 123–125

While the missionaries in Allahabad and Agra had found refuge within the forts of these cities, their hearts were full of anxiety concerning their dear missionary friends in Futtehgurh. The tidings that came at length were of the saddest. A boat had been secured in which they thought it possible they might escape to Cawnpore; but before they embarked they gathered around them the little band of Christian natives, and Mr. Campbell addressed them, telling them that while they themselves entertained but faint hopes that they could escape the vengeance of their enemies, the Christians, who were natives of the country, might perhaps find refuge in the villages; and for their further encouragement he said, "I know that the Church of Christ in India will remain, and that even the gates of hell shall not prevail against it. A final farewell it proved, for the boat upon which the true-hearted band embarked, bore them to their death." [30]

We can observe that Mr. Campbell's predictions (dare we call it prophesy?) have come true, for the Church of Christ in India has remained, and though Christians are still very much in the minority, it grows stronger and stronger every day through the prayers of God's people.

For a record of the details of the fate of Albert and Amanda and the other missionaries and children on their station we can look to the memoirs of Albert's younger brother and his wife, William and Rachel Johnson, who, devastated by the sacrifice of Albert and Amanda, came forward to take their place in North India.

Rachel was lost to a tragic accident in 1888 in Charlotte, North Carolina, where William had been president of Biddle University for five years in an interval from their work in India. After she died,

---

[30] Ibid. pp. 125–126

as soon as their other children were settled, William and his older daughter, Mary, returned to serve in India until his death in 1926.[31]

> According to the editor of Rachel's letters, "Albert's and Amanda's letters first reflected alarm about the mutiny when they learned that Delhi had been burned and "insurgents" were marching, 5,000 strong with an army of 'thieves and plunderers, on Agra, eighty miles from their home. Lines of communication with the outside world were quickly closed. Another missionary couple sharing their station, the Campbells, with their two small children, returned with Albert and Amanda to join two other missionary couples in Fattehgurh. As the story was pieced together later, 116 British soldiers, civil servants and merchant families, as well as the four American missionary couples and the two Campbell children, boarded boats and set sail down the Ganges River toward Kanpur on June 4.
> They headed toward what they thought would be a sanctuary in Kanpur, the home of the raja (king) of the area, Nana Sahib, a graduate of the Government College who professed to admire everything English. Many of the British leaders from Fattegurh had been frequent guests in his home, gone hunting with him, and otherwise enjoyed his hospitality. But when the fleeing foreigners finally reached what they thought was friendly territory, they were greeted with a roar of artillery which killed a British woman, a child and an ayah, (nurse maid). In confusion, the passengers left the boats to hide in the tall grass.

---

[31] *Affectionately, Rachel, letters from India edited by Barbara Mitchell Tull,* (Kent, Ohio and London: The Kent State University Press), pp. 14, 340

Soon an army of sepoys gathered up the prisoners, tied them together two by two, and marched them off to Nana Sahib, who had assumed leadership of the mutinous sepoys (Indians serving in the British army) in Kanpur.

Nana Sahib was in a dilemma. He was head of a Maratha Confederation which had ruled much of India before the turn of the century. Now he was being challenged to demonstrate where his primary loyalties lay; with the foreigners or with his own people. In his zeal to leave no doubt about his decision, Nana Sahib entered the British history of the revolt as the 'incarnation of brutality and treachery'. Among those giving counsel to Nana Sahib were advisors who suggested letting the merchants, planters, teachers, and missionaries go. But the voices that prevailed said, "No, let the unclean foreigners be rooted out." When the British offered the sepoys 300,000 rupees ($150,000) for release of the captives, the response was, "It is blood we want, not money."

Thus, Albert and Amanda and the other bound prisoners were prodded, ridiculed, and marched for a day and a half toward the military station in Kanpur. At 7:00 a.m, June 13, 1857, the prisoners were taken out of the house and marched to the parade ground. There they were shot.[32]

The missionaries had placed their hope of refuge in Kanpur because Nana Sahib had been a friend and gracious host to them and the British before the rebellion. But they were brutally betrayed.

---

[32] Ibid. pp. 15–17

Kanpur (or Cawnpore as it was spelled before India's independence) is the city where Frank and Esther Fiol, my husband's parents, served from 1939 to 1980. The church Frank pastored for many years is located in that military area (or cantonment, as the British say) where the atrocity occurred. Across the street from the Bible Presbyterian Church mentioned in the Frank Fiols' memoirs, stands the Anglican Church. On the walls of that church the names of those who died are written, Albert's and Amanda's among them. On one of our visits to Kanpur, I went to search out those names and spent some time mourning those young lives lost so early in their missionary endeavors.

I am told that in 1857, during the mutiny, Nana Sahib's troops were quartered in what was to become the Bible Presbyterian Church building. From these quarters, Nana's troops were able to see across the street to the larger Anglican Church where many English people had gone for refuge. The well at the Anglican Church was in the rifle sights of these Indian troops so that any English person going to draw water could be shot. This took place in the hottest months of the year in North India when water is most important for survival.

When the British again gained control in 1857, Nana Sahib disappeared and perhaps spent the rest of his life in Nepal, though nobody knows for sure where he fled.

It was almost a century later, shortly after the Scottish regiment and all British troops had left India in 1947, that the property was given to the Bible Presbyterian Church that David's father and mother had planted. It is not only an active church today but a training center for Christian workers. [33]

Nana Sahib and his associates have been acclaimed as "Freedom Fighters." There is a park honoring him in Kanpur. There is also a memorial in the same park honoring the British men, women, and children, as well as American missionaries and their children, who died during that mutiny.

---

[33] *Mission Miracles, Memoirs of Frank and Esther Fiol, The Early Years and Ministry in Kanpur.*

Today many of your missionaries are serving in different political situations or other types of upheavals such as the covid-19 pandemic of 2020. Keep your eye on the areas where they are located and note when they might be in danger from political conflict. Ask the Lord to protect them, to give them wisdom as to when to retreat, and to give them discretion in discussing (or not discussing) political matters. Pray that their nationalities will not be held against them and that they will have the wisdom to know how to keep the love of Christ central in their associations and conversations.

Pray that they will be guided to live out and share the Gospel and be able to rely on the Sovereign Lord to be with them; that they will be willing to glorify His name in any way He sees fit when they get into tough situations, even unto a martyr's death, if it is God's plan to give them that honor.

Another way missionaries feel betrayed is when those in whose lives they have invested, institutions or individuals, stray from the faith and even set out to do harm to the work. In the case where the home we were involved with found its funding agency transformed from a friend to an enemy, referred to in chapter 2, a few people who had grown up in the home joined in the verbal attack against it. They were among those telling lies and making the home and its employees look bad. But it is our prayer that they have repented and realized that God's truth will prevail, and His work cannot be thwarted.

Even in the church, as Paul mentions in 1 Timothy 1:19, 20, some will reject good conscience and faith and "suffer shipwreck." Of the seed of the Word of God that is sown in the parable found in Matthew 13:20–23, we are warned to expect that some will receive the Word of God with joy but fall away later. And in falling away it seems that some will betray those who have invested in them, as in the case of Judas.

This can be extremely demoralizing for your missionaries and their fellow workers. Pray that it may not happen. But if it does, ask that the missionaries will be able to respond in love and pray for those straying, remembering that His Spirit is grieved as well. Pray that those who have invested in those lives will be assured that their labor has not been in vain.

On a lighter side, the people of some cultures tend to be a bit more careless with the truth than we are comfortable with. One day I went to a neighborhood shop to make a phone call. This would have been in the 90s before cell phones took over the country; even before home phones were worth having. But you could pay your money to a shopkeeper who would provide his shop phone as a service to the public, if you didn't mind waiting in line.

It was a very interesting wait you would have because you couldn't help but listen to the conversations going on before your turn came. When I was waiting in line that day, the shopkeeper himself was on the phone. He was saying, "Oh, well I'm not sure that I can do that. I would like to, but—oh no, the lights just went out. I'm afraid I can't." Now it would not have been unusual at all for the electricity to have failed and everything to have grown dark, but the lights were still shining brightly as he hung up. I remember thinking as I walked home, *How often have I been lied to without realizing it?*

When I was shopping for something, I knew that it is often not safe to believe what I was told. But it was very hard if I really wanted that item. I so badly wanted to believe what they were telling me about it.

Many times I have invited a lady to church and been quite hopeful that she would come because she definitely said she would. Sometimes I would stand at the gate or at the back of the church through half of the service, waiting for her. She very rarely showed up. I sometimes wondered if even when she said she would come she did not intend to, possibly even when she made the promise she knew she wouldn't be there. People are so eager to say what they think you want them to say. When you are out of sight, it doesn't seem to matter anymore. I now smile indulgently when a new worker says, "They said they would come to church, I'll wait outside for them." It may be a long wait. But you never know when they just might come, so I don't discourage anyone.

Pray...

- ...for discernment for your missionaries, that they be neither gullible nor cynical.
- ...that their own distinction between truth and falsehood will not be blurred.
- ...that they will never be found betraying the trust of anyone.
- ...that they "will be delivered from perverse and evil men;—." **II Thes. 3:2**
- ...that they will be protected in the midst of political turmoil or persecution and will have wisdom to know when to stay and when to flee.
- ...for grace for them to face whatever the Lord ordains for them.
- ...for the stability of the governments where they are working.
- ...that they will not be discouraged.

CHAPTER 6
~ ~ Great Influence, Unintended Consequences~ ~

Lottie Moon

Charlotte (Lottie) Moon was born in 1840 to a land and slave-holding family near Charlottesville, Virginia. The Civil War broke out a few weeks after she graduated from college. Due to a number of factors, including early death of husbands, deprivation of the war, and loss of slave help after the war, the women in her family were of necessity strong and educated. Her father died in1853, but in his will he provided for the education of his five daughters as well as his two sons, and her mother saw that they received it.

After attending finishing school, she enrolled in September 1857, in the brand-new college called Albemarle Female Institute, established by the Baptist Church of Charlottesville. It was the first opportunity for women of the south to study the same courses that the men studied at the University of Virginia. It was here that Lottie came to know the Lord after having been rebellious and wanting to go her own way for a time.[34]

Lottie was a Southern Baptist. In 1845, mainly because the northern church would not send slave owners to the mission field, the new Southern Baptist denomination had been formed.

By the late 1860s, Southern Baptist leaders in the church had begun to ponder the place of southern women in light of the economic and social changes that the Civil War had brought to the region. Single women, of whom there were many since great numbers of men had died in the war, began feeling called to serve in home and foreign missions. Married women had been going with their husbands to the mission fields but apart from one exception that didn't work out, single women were not sent. It was considered that they would have a hard time managing without a "man to lean on."

Lottie made her voice heard in the matter by writing articles in *The Religious Herald,* arguing that "women should be allowed to do paid religious work." She rejected the idea that women's religious work should be limited. She argued that "women could make it their business to minister to the poor and suffering, establish Sunday Schools, sewing schools, night schools and mothers' meetings.— Scores never enter a church for want of decent clothing—-How are such people to be reached then? Evidently, the gospel message must be carried to their homes, and actual trial has shown that women are peculiarly fitted for just this kind of work. Our Lord does not call on women to preach, or to pray in public, but no less does he say to them than to men, 'Go, work today in my vineyard.'"[35]

Lottie looked for every opportunity to serve the poor and tell them of the Gospel. She became a teacher. In 1872, Lottie's younger sister, Edmonia (Eddie), and Lula Whilden became the first single

---

[34] Janet Benge and Geoff Benge, *Lottie Moon: Giving Her All for China* (Seattle, WA: YWAM Pub., 2001), pp 1-23

[35] Regina D. Sullivan, *Lottie Moon: a Southern Baptist Missionary to China in History and Legend* (Baton Rouge: Louisiana State University Press, 2011), p. 46,

women sent out under the mission board's revised policy to send single women in pairs or attached to missionary families. Eddie went to work with Tarlton and Martha Crawford, Southern Baptist missionaries, in Tengchow, Shantung province, China. Lottie and a friend, Anna Safford, a Presbyterian, were committed to teaching in a school, so Lottie felt she could not leave at that time. But by September 1, 1873, both Lottie and Anna were on their way to China; Lottie to join her sister, "Eddie," and the Crawfords, and Anna to join a Presbyterian mission.[36] Until 1912, for thirty-nine years, Lottie worked faithfully in China at doing the things "women could make it their business to do," often pleading for more money to be raised and more missionaries to be sent to China.

The Lord allowed Lottie to avoid break down in health (which called her sister home), and endure over work, plague, famine, political rebellions, disagreements among missionaries, and other factors that took out many missionaries. This, along with the social standing of her family, her prolific articles in Baptist publications, the fact that she was one of the first women to receive a university education and that her teachers became leaders in the Southern Baptist Church, made her a high profile person in that denomination and in the development of their policies.[37]

Lottie was on the scene at a key time in the history of missions in the US when most denominations were grappling with the issues of raising money for missions, the development of methods that would encourage self-support rather than dependence among the nationals, and the establishment of the place of women in missions and in the church. The circumstances and timing of her death were to have long-lasting effects on the church as well, as we shall see later.

In 1903 at the age of sixty-two, Lottie went on furlough. It had been ten years since her last furlough, and the board had made the policy that their missionaries should take a furlough after every ten years. She saw it as an opportunity to raise the money needed for a new hospital. Many people urged her to not return after that

---

[36] Ibid, p. 49
[37] Ibid, pp. 117, 118

furlough. Her thirty years of toil in China had taken its toll on her physically. But her heart and her home were now in China, and after thirteen months, she went back to her original station in Shangtung province. The hospital was built in Hwanghsien. Lottie had decided that her place was in education since after the upheaval of the Boxer Rebellion, the people were inclined to leave their old ways and look to the education of the children. She established and administered several schools.

A number of new missionaries had been sent to Tengchow. A theological school had been started, but soon it was felt wise to move the school to Hwanghsien near the hospital, and most of the missionaries went with it. Lottie remained in Tengchow. Her home had become a center for many Christians who came in from the villages where there had been much preaching of the Gospel, and she would not leave that ministry.

There are two versions of the cause of her death in 1912. The first appears in my first source, *Lottie Moon, Giving Her All for China*, by Janet & Geoff Benge. Two of their three sources were published by the Women's Missionary Union of the Southern Baptist Church. Their version follows:

By 1912, China saw the end of a bloody revolution during which Lottie labored faithfully in the hospital for ten days, single-handedly caring for casualties of both sides. The other missionaries had evacuated to another city but did return at Lottie's example. The people were still suffering from drought and famine as well.

Appeals to the mission board for financial help revealed that they had no funds to help. "Given the crisis, Lottie decided that every penny not spent on her was a penny she could give to help someone in need. Her old cook still made meals, but Lottie preferred to go out into the yard and give her portion of food to some passing emaciated child rather than eat it herself. Slowly, and without anyone realizing it, Lottie Moon was beginning to starve herself so that she could feed others. By the time one of her fellow missionaries noticed what she was doing, Lottie weighed only fifty pounds."

When the other missionaries became aware of this, they took her to the hospital. After several weeks, they decided she should be taken back to the United States (against her will) to recover. Cynthia Miller, a missionary nurse, accompanied her. Lottie died on the way on Christmas Eve, 1912.[38]

A second version of the circumstances surrounding her death is found in *Lottie Moon, A Southern Baptist Missionary to China, History and Legend* by Regina D. Sullivan, published by Louisiana State University Press. It references a large number of primary and secondary sources including personal letters and diaries of missionaries. According to this version, the facts concerning the revolution, drought and famine are accurate, but not those that claim she gave all of her money and food and starved herself to feed the victims of the famine.

In early 1912, she was disappointed to find that her request for new missionaries to cover the work for a furlough she planned in 1913 was not likely to be granted because of lack of funds. They could expect no financial help for famine relief either. She was planning to stay on until other workers could be sent. In August 1912, she penned her final letter to the board, which was published. It showed that her mind was agile and she was fully engaged in her work.

> In September Dr. James and Annie Gaston traveled from Laichow (Lauzhou) to visit Moon. They spent a few days in her home, where they found her healthy and well. Soon after this visit, however, Moon's mental and physical condition began to deteriorate rapidly. The Gastons had noted nothing aberrant in her behavior, yet, by early October, Moon's Tengchow coworkers became concerned at her increasingly strange conduct.

---

[38] Janet Benge and Geoff Benge, *Lottie Moon: Giving Her All for China* (Seattle, WA: YWAM Pub., 2001), pp. 106-125

Moon had sent a message to W. W. Adams to return immediately from the countryside where he was preaching.

> When he arrived, he found Moon in a "troubled state of mind." She told Adams that she had over-drawn her bank account, but, when he checked, Adams found that she had funds to her credit. Unable to convince Moon of this fact, he offered to loan her money. When she seemed to regain rational thought, Adams returned to the villages. A few days later, other missionaries realized that Moon was not herself. Jane Lide and Bonnie Turner went to her home and found that she was unable to care for herself. They made plans to move Moon to Lide's home, and they sent for Jessie Pettigrew, a missionary nurse based in Hwanghien, to come to Tengchow immediately and assess Moon's condition. When she arrived, Pettigrew found Moon had lost her appetite and had not been eating properly. She was thin and weak. Pettigrew also discovered a large boil eating through the flesh on Moon's neck behind her ear. Pettigrew treated it, but she found she could not treat the most disturbing change in Moon's condition—her dementia. When Pettigrew asked what was wrong, Moon replied, "it's my mind, troubles in my mind.

The rest of the story matches with the first account. She, with a companion, set sail for the United States, and Lottie died on the way. [39]

No doubt Lottie did give her all for the people of China, but the cause of her death does not seem to have been starvation. Somehow

---

[39] Regina D. Sullivan, *Lottie Moon: a Southern Baptist Missionary to China in History and Legend* (Baton Rouge: Louisiana State University Press, 2011), p. 160

the facts became distorted, but according to Sullivan, after Lottie's demise, the report that she had starved herself for the people of China because of lack of funds from the States was very effective for raising money among the people of her homeland who knew and loved her and her work.

Consider the issues that were facing the Southern Baptist church in Lottie's day, for your missionaries today are facing the same problems still, in varying degrees.

Raising money is often a big hurtle for a person to get over when considering whether or not to go to the mission field. In Lottie's situation, the money was all raised by the mission board or church, though she did seem to have some personal resources that she used from time to time. Missionaries would not be sent until the church had enough money to guarantee their passage and salary. If a missionary ran into a need on the field—the church, the mission board, or the Women's Missionary Union—after it was formed partly through Lottie's encouragement, had to raise the money. At the time when she appealed for famine relief and new missionaries to carry on the work so that she could go on a furlough planned for 1913, the board not only didn't have money to send, it was in debt. This issue has been discussed in Chapter 3, page 45.

Self-support. In Lottie's day, one of her senior missionaries, Tarlton Crawford, became more and more devoted to the concept of "self-support." To him that meant that not missionaries but nationals should provide their own support for institutions like schools and hospitals and seminaries as well as for churches. He felt that helping them with money would make them "dependent upon foreign funds" (as we would describe it today). He eventually began to feel that missionaries should do nothing more than evangelize. He insisted that the development of churches, schools, or hospitals should be entirely up to the Chinese. He was a very domineering person and had much influence on younger missionaries, Lottie included. He even tried to force his views on the whole denomination. Eventually he left the Southern Baptists and formed a mission of his own. Crawford's policy of evangelizing without consideration for social needs did not bring the desired results.

Later in her ministry, Lottie went back to raising money to establish schools and a hospital. Many of the missionaries working with her in those years were nurses and doctors.[40]

In our days, it was always uppermost in our minds and those of the other missionaries that churches and other Christian institutions should become as financially independent as possible. Whatever could be done to that end was done. We rarely raised money to help churches, though we ourselves were members of the churches and contributed as such. We did not want the churches to be dependent on foreign funds.

But the institutions had to be significantly financed from funds raised abroad in the beginning. As was said of Lottie Moon, we made self-support a goal, not a way of working. Gradually, we have seen them become able to generate their own finances in different ways.

We have worked hard to also ensure that the pastors and administrators of the churches and institutions are for the most part nationals and not missionaries. Missionaries and nationals together have started institutions, but our goal was always to, at the appropriate time, turn them over to national leadership completely. The Lord has sent the qualified national personnel necessary as a result of much prayer. We praise His name. Westerners sometimes play supporting roles as volunteers.

The role of women. The struggle that the churches had in Lottie's time over this issue has definitely benefitted all of Christian missions since that time. So much important, wonderful work in missions has been done by strong, brave women of faith, like Lottie, single and married, answering the call of the Lord to go into all the world with the Gospel.

One thing I was impressed to see no mention of in either of my sources for Lottie's life was conflict between single and married women. Married women can be tempted to resent the fact that single women are working closely with their husbands while they are

---

[40] Regina D. Sullivan, *Lottie Moon: a Southern Baptist Missionary to China in History and Legend* (Baton Rouge: Louisiana State University Press, 2011), pp. 70-71, 132-147

looking after the babies at home. They might feel jealous of the recognition given to the single women while their own hard work and sacrifice are often overlooked. Single women are sometimes tempted to be jealous of married women or to think that they aren't doing their fair share of the work.

But the friendship between Lottie and Martha Crawford and their partnership in the work is extremely touching. There is no record that I saw of tension between them like there was between other missionaries or between Lottie's sister and the Crawfords. Martha would go out and help in the evangelistic work when she could. Lottie would in fact call her when she couldn't handle it herself. In the later years, after Tarlton Crawford died, Martha came back to the mission and worked with Lottie.

In all of the tensions between missionaries, which are bound to be there, Lottie and Martha seem to have worked hard to keep peace. They were truly "strong" women.

Unfortunately, the result of the very worthy causes of organizing the women of the denomination to raise money for missions, and of freeing women to do effective mission work, caused friction between the women and the leadership of the denomination.

I doubt that Lottie would have been pleased to know that in years to come the issue of the place of women in the Lord's work would be associated with the attack of the enemy on the authority of the Word of God[41] in many denominations. I am confident that she herself gave her all in proclaiming the Gospel and the Word in China with full faith that the Bible is inerrant and our guide and authority. She was a wonderful example for all believers, men as well as women.

PRAY...

- ...that your missionaries will be able to raise their support quickly; that they will enjoy telling churches and individuals what God is doing and giving others opportunity to have a part in it through praying and giving.

---

[41] Eleanor Fiol, "The Glory of the Christian Woman"

- …that they will have wisdom in investing money in the work with the goal of making it self-supporting.
- …for wisdom for denominational authorities and mission boards as they make policies regarding missions, that they will be those that will give the support and guidance needed as the missionaries follow the leading of the Lord.
- …for missionaries as they have differing ideas about the best methods of working, that they will respect each other and not be dogmatic.
- …for occasions when such differences will necessitate a change in location or relationships, that it will be done quietly and cause as little disruption in the Lord's work as possible.
- …that your missionaries and those guiding and supporting them will be dedicated to being peace-makers.
- …that your women missionaries will know the joy and glory of being women following God's plan for womanhood as revealed in the Word of God.

CHAPTER 7
~ ~ *A New Way* ~ ~

Sadhu Sundar Singh

You may not have heard of the missionary of this chapter, though Christians in India hold him in the highest regard. Early in the twentieth century, when Amy Carmichael was beginning her ministry in South India, he baffled and then amazed the missionaries in North India and soon caught the attention of the whole world in a long robe and bare feet. Christians in Dehra Dun, the capital of the State of Uttar Khand in the foothills of the Himalaya Mountains, honor Sadhu Sundar Singh, or The Sadhu as he is sometimes called, every year in a conference devoted to competitive debating and musical competition. I suspect that he is remembered in conferences through-out India.

Sadhu Sundar Singh was born in North India in 1889 to a Sikh family in the Punjab. "Sikh" means learner or disciple. It is a name given to one of orthodox Hinduism's breakaway sects, founded in the fifteenth century by Guru Nanak who was followed by nine other gurus or teachers. Sikhs deny idolatry and most of the rites of the Hindu religion and seek a purer form of worship along the lines of devotion to God. [42]

Sikhs are known for the turbans worn by the men.

> The turban as well as the other articles of faith worn by Sikhs have an immense spiritual as well as temporal significance. The symbolisms of wearing a turban are many—it being regarded as a symbol of sovereignty, dedication, self-respect, courage and piety, but the reason all practicing Sikhs wear the turban is just one—out of love and obedience to the wishes of the founders of their faith.[43]

Sundar learned much from his devout mother. She was a refined and gifted lady, very broad-minded in her sympathies. She was on friendly terms with the American Presbyterian Mission ladies and permitted their visits to her home. The relationship between Sundar and his mother was deep and tender. He was the youngest of the family and seldom left her side. She would often say to him, "You must not be careless and worldly like your brothers. You must seek peace of soul and love religion, and some day you must become a holy sadhu."

---

[42] T. E. Riddle, *The Vision and the Call, the Life of Sadhu Sundar Singh*, (Overseas Missions Committee, Presbyterian Church of New Zealand), pp. 4-5

[43] "Sikh Theology Why Sikhs Wear a Turban," Gurduwara, n.d., http://igurud-wara.com/wp-content/uploads/2016/02/Sikh-Theology-Why-Sikhs-wear-a-Turban.pdf)

But at the age of fourteen, Sunder lost this dearest earthly friend. The biographer writes, "How he missed her gentle companionship no one knows, but today when he speaks of her, his voice grows tender and his eyes look sad. He believes that were she alive she would be satisfied to see him living and working as he is this day."[44]

As a boy, Sundar was sent to a Christian school where he strongly felt that Christianity was a false religion and at first joined with other boys in ridiculing the Christians. But soon he stopped that and began listening to the message of the Bible. He was sometimes seen conversing with a Christian teacher. "The leaven of the gospel had entered his heart, and as he read John 3:16 a whisper of comfort came to his heart. But still, the burden of anguish prevented him from finding rest."[45]

On December 18, 1904, when he was fifteen, his life was changed. In his own words in one of his addresses, he described his dilemma:

> I was faithful to my own religion but I could not get any satisfaction or peace——So I thought of leaving it all and committing suicide. Three days after I had burnt a Bible, I woke up about three o'clock in the morning, had my usual bath, and prayed, "O God, if there is a God, wilt though show me the right way or I will kill myself." My intention was that, if I got no satisfaction, I would place my head upon the railway line when the 5 o'clock train passed by and kill myself. If I got no satisfaction in this life, I thought I would get it in the next. I was praying and praying but got no answer; and I prayed for half an hour longer hoping to get peace.

---

[44] Mrs. Arthur Parker, *Sadhu Sundar Singh*, (The Christian Literature Society, 1918), p. 9

[45] Ibid. p. 12

At 4:30 a.m. I saw something of which I had no idea at all previously. In the room where I was praying I saw a great light. I thought the place was on fire. I looked round, but could find nothing. Then the thought came to me that this might be an answer that God had sent me. Then as I prayed and looked into the light, I saw the form of the Lord Jesus Christ. It had such an appearance of glory and love. If it had been some Hindu incarnation I would have prostrated myself before it. But it was the Lord Jesus Christ whom I had been insulting a few days before. I felt that a vision like this could not come out of my own imagination. I heard a voice saying in Hindustani "How long will you persecute me? I have come to save you; you were praying to know the right way. Why do you not take it?"

The thought then came to me, "Jesus Christ is not dead but living and it must be He Himself." O I fell at His feet and got this wonderful Peace which I could not get anywhere else. This is the joy I was wishing to get. This was heaven itself. When I got up, the vision had all disappeared; but although the vision disappeared the Peace and Joy have remained with me ever since.

Though his father had taught him to respect all religions, and especially their holy books, having his son openly profess another religion was completely unacceptable. Sundar's family—father, uncle, older brother—made every effort to dissuade him from becoming a Christian, promising wealth and reminding him of their social position. He was not moved from his resolve by their pleading and reminding him of the shame that would come upon the family.

During this time, he found it so difficult to live at home that he made his way to the headquarters of the American Presbyterian Mission in Ludhiana where the missionaries took care of him. Special arrangements were made for the cooking of his food to please his family, and he entered the high school there. But he was disappointed to find that the other boys were only nominal Christians, and he could not live with their conduct. His situation had caused him to grow up far beyond their years of maturity. So he returned home.

After his family had tried to change him for a full nine months, when finally even the appeal of a friendly raja (local ruler) failed to move him, he was disowned and ordered to depart forever.

He considered his first night sleeping under a tree "my first night in heaven. I remember the wonderful joy that made me compare that time with the time when I was living in a luxurious home. In the midst of luxuries and comfort I could not find peace in my heart. The presence of the savior changed the suffering into peace."[46][47]

About the same time, a friend of Sundar's also had professed Christ. His parents brought a court case against the headmaster of the school, claiming that he had forced their son to become a Christian. The boy bravely stood up in court, held up a New Testament and declared, "Not because of the Padri Sahib (pastor) but by reading this I believe on Christ, so let the Padri Sahib go." Eventually, the school had to be closed, and the small group of Christians in the village, who were no longer permitted to buy food there, had to move to a friendlier place. This had left Sundar alone with his family.

The next day after being cast out, as Sundar sat in the train, the thought came to him that in Ropur there was a little colony of Christians, some of whom had lived in his town. Stepping out of the train, he made his way to the house of the kind Indian pastor and his wife. It was by the providence of God that Sundar did this, for very soon after his arrival, he fell violently ill. A deadly poison had been mixed in the food given him before he left home. His friend, also poisoned by his parents, did not survive.

A physician was called who declared he would surely die. "But as he lay, there came to him the profound belief that God had not called

[46] B. H. Streeter and A. J. Appasamy, *The Message of Sadhu Sundar Singh* (New York: The Macmillan Company, 1922), pp. 6-10.

[47] Mrs. Arthur Parker, *Sadhu Sundar Singh*, (The Christian Literature Society, 1918), p. 15-20

him out of darkness to die without witnessing to his faith in Christ, so he began to pray with all his remaining powers." In the morning the doctor returned and was amazed to find the boy alive. The doctor then began reading the New Testament, became a believer, and eventually went as a missionary to Burma.

When he was well enough to travel, Sundar went back to the missionaries in Ludhiana. But more attempts were made by his family to influence him, and the missionaries sent him farther away to the American Medical Mission in Sabathu near Simla in the Himalayan foothills. He was baptized at the Anglican Church there.

Sundar had long felt drawn to the life of a sadhu (roving holy man), and knowing what such a life involved, he willingly made the final sacrifice for it. His books and personal belongings were soon disposed of, and on October 6, 1905, just thirty-three days after his baptism, at the age of sixteen, he adopted the simple saffron robe that was to mark him for all time as one vowed to a religious life. With bare feet and no visible means of support, but with his New Testament in his hand and his Lord at his side, Sadhu Sundar Singh set out on the evangelistic campaign that lasted the rest of his life.

His very first place of ministry was in his own village, from which he had been driven only a short time previously. In every street, he bore faithful witness to the power of the Savior. He went from house to house, telling the women also the wonderful story. Then he visited the villages round about and went on toward Afghanistan and Kashmir. He suffered cold and privations along the way and in very few places was his message received. His sadhu's clothes gave him entrance everywhere, but often when it was discovered that he was a Christian, he was driven away. [48]

Soon he felt a burden for Tibet and went many times in his life to that country, beginning in 1908 when he was nineteen, to preach the Gospel at great peril to his life. It was necessary for him to traverse high mountains to get there, plodding on through the snow and bitter cold in bare feet, and to face the hostility of the people them-

---

[48] Mrs. Arthur Parker, *Sadhu Sundar Singh,* (The Christian Literature Society, 1918, p. 15-20

selves. They were Buddhists, who would not tolerate anyone from a religion not their own. Their religious leaders, called lamas, were especially dangerous. They had produced many Christian martyrs.

On the first trip, he started out alone, but God provided two Moravian missionaries at Poo, a frontier town, who gave him some instructions and a worker to accompany him for some distance and help him learn the language. He had the opportunity to witness to a good number of people.

Many are the stories of his persecution and deliverance in the land of Tibet. He visited often in the summer seasons until 1929 when he disappeared on his way to Tibet and was finally presumed dead at the age of forty.

But the ministry of this young, charming Indian in saffron robes was not confined to North India or Tibet. What he expected would be a brief visit to South India ended in a tour of that section of India, where St. Thomas is well honored and reported to have established the first church in the country. That trip lasted months. He was called to speak to huge crowds at the typical Indian conventions or rallies, giving his testimony and, among other things, charging the church of the south with the responsibility of taking the Gospel message to the north of India.

From there, he was called to Rangoon, Singapore, and Penang, where he came into contact with Chinese, Japanese, Malayans, Europeans, and Indians. Then he went on to China and Japan.

After more time in India and Tibet, he was called to minister, during numerous trips, in England, the United States, Australia, Germany, Switzerland, Sweden, Norway, Denmark, and Holland. Wherever he went, he mixed with and ministered to all Christians, for he had no time for what he called "isms." But always he would return to India and his mission field of Tibet.

Sundar himself had no desire to establish a following of Christian sadhus. He felt that would muddy the waters eventually. Some did emulate his lifestyle in doing Christian work as sadhus but not under his tutelage.

Sundar had told a missionary friend before he left for Tibet on what turned out to be his last journey, "If you do not hear from me before the end of July, you may just consider that I have gone to be with my Lord." When he did not return, several missionaries went to search for him.

No trace was found of the Sadhu and it was concluded that he may have died of small pox along with many other pilgrims on the trail that year. If such was the case, his remains would have been committed to the Ganges River. Some felt that it was a good thing that his body was not found, because he was held in such high esteem that his tomb most likely would have become a shrine had he been buried in India.

How does this inspire us to pray for our present missionaries? Each generation of new missionaries goes to the field having been taught, or developing themselves, ideas about how the work should be done. This is good and should be done. But God is not bound to follow our ideas. He will do His work in His way, especially in people of cultures that are different from ours. He may surprise us. Your missionaries will need to have discernment to recognize what is truly of the Lord and what is not.

When the boy, Sundar, did not adjust to the missionary school, most missionaries did not give up on him. They were able to see that God was doing something special in his life. They supported him as much as possible, which I believe is most commendable. They recognized the work of God in him and took advantage of his ministry to enrich their own.

There will be variations in methods of working that your missionaries will need to accept, and there will be certain movements or persons from whom it will be best for them to distance themselves for good reasons. Pray that they will know the difference. Pray that they will agree among themselves.

George Verwer, in his book, *Out of the Comfort Zone*, includes a chapter entitled, "A Grace-Awakened Approach to Missions Work." He quotes Charles Swindoll in his book, *The Grace Awakening*:

> …once we grasp grace's vertical significance as a free gift from God, much of horizontal grace— our extending it to others—automatically falls into place.

Verwer says, "There is such a need for this grace-awakened, big-hearted approach in mission work. There are so many areas where a lack of grace causes hurt and tension and positively hinders the work of God across the globe. So often our fellowship as Christians seems to be based more on minor areas in which we are like-minded, than on the real basics of the Gospel and the clear doctrines of the Christian faith which are so amazing and on which we should be more united.

The last twenty-five years of our ministry were spent aiding nationals in doing the work to which God had called them. We were involved at a seminary and in a school that was started primarily for the children of national workers. The people we were helping were all committed to spreading the good news of Jesus Christ, Son of God and Savior, as presented by the revelation of God in the Bible. They may not have done the work in the way that we might have if we had been put in their position. And they may not have always agreed with us in certain interpretations of the Bible, but they were building the kingdom/church on the same foundation that we were. We were sure that God had called us to support them.

In countries where Christians are so much in the minority, we believers know how much we need each other. We stick together. Minor issues that divide Christians into denominations are kept in the background. Any who are preaching the Gospel according to the Word of God are valued fellow workers.

Pray that your missionaries will be prepared to suffer for Christ—small inconveniences as well as serious persecution. Western culture puts great emphasis on comfort and the avoidance of all suffering. Christ has called us to suffer. He said, "as the Father has sent me, so send I you." Jesus was sent to suffer and die for us. We must be ready to do the same for Him if He should require it. The Sadhu seemed almost to have a longing to suffer for Christ. He seemed to "count it all joy" when he was persecuted, as though he loved to repay His Lord for the way He suffered for him.

PRAY...

- ...that your missionaries will understand how to extend that "horizontal grace".
- ...that they will have discernment to recognize the work of God in unusual ways in the nationals where they are working.
- ...that they will be able to discern also when they should distance themselves from methods or teachings that are unscriptural.
- ...that the Lord will use nationals touched by your missionaries' work to reach other nationals whom missionaries could not influence.
- ...that your missionaries will themselves be and will allow others to be "all things to all men that they might by all means save some" (I Corinthians 9:22).
- ...that your missionaries will be prepared to suffer for Christ.

CHAPTER 8
~ ~ *Get Used to It* ~ ~

Amy Carmichael

Life is a series of adjustments. We have all experienced them. From making the shocking transition out of the comfort of our mothers' wombs to drinking from a cup and going to kindergarten, through college, marriage, having a baby in the house, then two, three, etc., having sons and daughters-in-laws and becoming grandparents. Until we enter hospice and go on to be with the Lord, we are repeatedly having to adjust.

So it should not be difficult for us to relate to the many extra adjustments missionaries are called on to undergo along with all of those listed above. We should have no problem "reading between the lines," figuring out what their feelings might be and relating to them as we pray.

Amy Carmichael, born in 1868 in Northern Ireland, comes to mind in this regard. She is well known for her writings and for her ministry to little girls rescued from Indian temples. She is a good missionary example when it comes to the need for adjustment. She was one of seven children brought up in a strict Presbyterian family. Her father was a fairly well-to-do mill owner. She was well-read and especially loved poetry.[49]

Early in her life, Amy learned lessons on prayer. She and her two younger brothers were

> ...rowing a small boat in the long tidal channel near Portaberry where Grandmother Filson lived. The current caught the boat and swept it toward the open sea. Amy began to beseech God with a hymn: "He leadeth me, O blessed thought, O words with heavenly comfort fraught; Whate'er I do, where'er I be, still 'tis God's hand that leadeth me!" Frightened, Norman and Ernest joined in at the top of their lungs as their small arms cranked the oars against the current. Just as the rowboat seemed destined to cross the bar into the open sea, a coastguard lifeboat rescued them. God had surely answered Amy's plea. Life seemed lost, then found again, and Amy would never forget looking death in the face. But it was a good thing Norman and Ernest quickly forgot their brushes with death with their brash older sister, "or else they might not be so willing to follow me in my next adventure," she admitted. [50]

---

[49] Sam Wellman, *Amy Carmichael: Selfless Servant of India* (Uhrichville, OH: Barbour Pub., 2012), pp. 1–14

[50] Ibid. pp. 9–10

Another lesson on prayer had to do with the color of her eyes.

> She had prayed for blue eyes, "Please come and
> sit with me," she had said to Jesus as she did every
> night, smoothing a place on the sheet beside her.
> Welcoming Jesus into bed was her very first mem-
> ory—she had asked Jesus for blue eyes. Mother
> had said that Jesus hears our prayers and answers
> them. But no, in her mirror the next morning
> her eyes remained brown as dirt—"like a bright
> ray of the sun on a gloomy day she had realized
> His answer was No." That didn't make it any less
> disappointing. Her mother had eyes as blue as
> forget-me-nots. So did her brother. Maybe that
> disappointment explained her peculiar torment
> of him. For she would pinch him until the tears
> glistened in his angry eyes." This was perhaps
> her first adjustment to having God say no. She
> would have to 'get used to' brown eyes.[51]

Many years later. as she served in India. she realized that her
brown eyes were meant for a very special purpose. Since nearly all of
the eyes of those who looked to her as to a mother were brown, they
must have all the more treasured her as one of them.

In 1880, Amy was sent to study for four years in a Methodist
boarding school in Harrogate, England. She was very sad to leave
her happy childhood behind. But it was in her boarding school years
that her adventures for God began, though not until the end of her
time there. She often regretted that she had not applied herself to her
studies in those four years but tended to lead her schoolmates into
mischief. They described her as "wild Irish."

> In the spring of 1884, at 16 years of age, she sang
> in the choir at the meetings of the Children's

---

[51] Ibid. pp. 8–9

Special Service Mission a simple hymn, an import from America, that had become popular: Jesus Loves Me! This I know, for the Bible tells me so—. The first verse sang to Amy's heart like a thousand angels! Did she know she belonged to Jesus? The chorus spoke to her just as grandly. Jesus loved her. Of course, the Bible had told her that. But had she accepted that love? She knew by now how the Wesleys had stressed a second sanctification in a Christian's development. But it seemed mumbo jumbo to Amy. The last verse of the hymn resonated in her heart: Jesus loves me! He will stay close beside me all the way. Thou hast bled and died for me; I will henceforth live for Thee.

After the hymn, Mr. Arrowsmith asked the children to be silent for several minutes. Amy brooded. What if what the Wesleys had said was true? Was this her second chance? Did she have to "accept" Jesus? As far as she could remember, she had not once actually asked Jesus to come into her heart. The pain He bore on the cross seemed to crush her. Yes, she would open her heart to Jesus. Then it happened. Suddenly her chains fell away! She was soaring. The years in England that had seemed to her so empty, such a void, took on special meaning now. She had come into the desert as a pilgrim; and away from the distractions of human love at home, she had found God.[52]

Our missionaries will have different stories of how and when they came to know the Lord and committed their lives to serve Him. Pray that those stories will remain fresh in their hearts and minds as

[52] Sam Wellman, *Amy Carmichael: Selfless Servant of India* (Uhrichville, OH: Barbour Pub., 2012), pp. 20–21

they work to bring others to that dedication to the One who loves them and died for them. Pray that they will never forget that doing that is their ultimate goal.

The events of Amy's life between the time she came to know Jesus in 1880 until she went as a missionary to Japan are filled with adjustments to her new life in Christ and her calling as a missionary.

Upon returning to Scotland, she became aware of the plight of the poor when she noticed a little girl peering in the window of the tea shop where she and her mother were eating delicacies and realized that the little girl was hungry and cold. Later she wished she had urged her mother to invite her in and regretted that she was not doing something for such little girls. She prayed, "Please, God, tell me what to do."

One day on the way home she felt led, with the help of her brothers, to help an old lady with a big bundle, but as they were walking along with her, she became embarrassed at the thought of her peers seeing them with the lady. Then she clearly heard a voice say,

"Now if any man build upon this foundation gold, silver, precious stones, wood, hay, stubble; every man's work shall be made manifest: for the day shall declare it, because it shall be revealed by fire; and the fire shall try every man's work of what sort it is. If any man's work abide which he hath built thereupon, he shall receive a reward." She immediately recognized that God was speaking to her in the words of Scripture, 1 Corinthians 3:12–15. She was sure she had heard the voice that no one else had and she determined to immediately start offering her gold."

Amy began a work with the children of her neighborhood but soon realized that the poor children had more need of hearing about Jesus. She went into the slums and began a work with children and later with the "shawlies," a poor working class of women. That work had grown very large and spread to other cities before she left for the mission field. At the age of seventeen, she lost her father who was only fifty-four. But she continued her work, dressed in the somber colors of mourning.

From 1886 on, she attended yearly Keswick conventions where the main object of the teaching was sanctity and the subduing of the self. The Quaker, Robert Wilson, a coal tycoon, one of the founders of the Keswick meetings, became a good friend of her family. He introduced them to Frances Havergal's poetry and hymns.

One of the speakers at the Keswick meetings was Hudson Taylor, telling of the need of 865 million people in other lands to hear the Gospel, 50,000 dying every day unsaved. He told of William Carey's work in India. "When the Keswick Society decided to start the funding necessary to send forth missionaries sometime in the future, Amy found herself strangely excited."[53]

In 1890 she was invited to go to live with Robert Wilson and his sons and join them in the work in their Quaker Church. She was much gifted in working with children. In that two years of time with the Quakers, she continued her extensive reading habits—in the works of Brother Lawrence, Rutherford, Kempis, Bunyan, Spurgeon, as well as the English Mystics: Raymond Lully, Lady Julian of Norwich and Richard Rolle. "Many of her favorites had one thing in common: God had revealed Himself to the writer."

It was here that she learned from Robert Wilson,

> We must drop labels (of denominations). If our precious Lord came tomorrow, what use would we have of such labels?
>
> Amy had already begun to think similar thoughts. She had known Presbyterian ways from babyhood, but she had learned in Harrogate to appreciate the pious yearnings of Methodism. She had also learned to value the beautiful ritual of the Church of England. Now she would learn to enjoy the quietness of the Quakers and the earnest beliefs of the Baptists. Surely these were all good things, all meant to honor the Lord.[54]

---

[53] Ibid. p. 34

[54] Sam Wellman, *Amy Carmichael: Selfless Servant of India* (Uhrichville, OH: Barbour Pub., 2012), pp. 44, 45

She was adjusting to the diversity within God's kingdom. Amy was torn between the thought of the many who hadn't heard the Gospel on the one hand and the needs of her family and work in Ireland and Scotland on the other. But on the morning of January 14, 1892, she wrote to her mother listing the reasons that made her think she shouldn't go, including "my not being strong." She wrote, "But yesterday, I went to my room and just asked the Lord what it all meant, what did He wish me to do, and, Mother, as clearly as I ever heard you speak, I heard Him say, 'Go Ye.'"

Then came the adjustment to a different type of uncertainty. To what country was she to go and under what auspices? The Keswick Conference had raised funds, but it had no established work or sending agency. Robert Wilson set out to make her the first Keswick missionary and find a place for her.

You would think that after such a distinct call, the way would be smooth, but not so. They first thought she could go to work with a couple returning to China, but the plans of that couple suddenly changed. Next the China Inland Mission doctor would not approve her. Then exactly one year after her decision to go, she was struck by the thought that she should go to Japan. A contact was made with a mission in Japan, and before she even heard the reply, she insisted on sailing with three missionaries who were going to Shanghai. She would wait there for the reply! She could not "get used to" waiting for directions![55]

On the way, Amy had the opportunity of leading two people to Christ, one being the captain of the vessel, Sutlej. But she remembered the words of Robert Wilson, "If stone in the quarry is hammered again and again, which blow splits it? 'All of them,' you would say. And in the same way you must never say, 'I won that soul for Christ,' because it was won by the first witness for Christ and the last witness for Christ and all those in between!'"[56]

The morning of April 25, 1893, Amy arrived in Japan. Three needs for adjustment met her very quickly. First, she saw that the

[55] Ibid. pp. 45-57
[56] Ibid. p. 33

missionaries were squabbling among themselves. "Well, good heavens," said one woman indignantly to Amy when she mentioned it, "you didn't think all missionaries love each other, did you?"

"Actually, I did," replied Amy. But she was to find cause to do a bit of squabbling herself in her future work.

Secondly, she found that the missionaries at the station she was assigned to had chosen to ignore Hudson Taylor's policy of adopting the clothing and permissible customs of the targeted country. They were living in Japan much the same lifestyle that they would in England. They wore their English clothes, drank their English tea in the English way, etc., and Amy could not adjust to this attitude.

And thirdly, the Japanese language was a mystery to her. But she hoped that with practice she would be able to learn it. (You can never go wrong in praying for your missionaries as they struggle with the language of their country—or even the accent and vocabulary of a different English-speaking country).

She had to use an interpreter her whole time in Japan, much to her dislike, but gradually immersed herself in the Japanese culture, wearing Japanese clothing, eating Japanese food, appreciating their ways of doing things simply, traveling third class, and sleeping in their hotels or on the floor. She saw demons cast out of one man, and a good number converted. All of the missionaries in Matsuye began praying with her when they saw that people were coming to Christ and being added to the church through her ministry.

During this time in Japan, she reported that a few serious men had "eyed her as a wife." But she did not feel the need of a husband. She struggled then with a fear of loneliness in later life that she felt was from the devil. But when she asked the Lord about it, she felt He answered, "None of them that trust in me shall be desolate."[57]

Her time in Japan was to be short but fruitful. Soon after December 16, 1893, her twenty-sixth birthday, the "miraculous expansion" of people being added to the church through her ministry ended, and Amy's health deteriorated. She began to have severe

---

[57] Ibid. p. 67-68

headaches, a condition they called "Japanese Head." The only cure known was to leave Japan.

By July 28, 1894, she was on her way to answer a call for help from friends in Ceylon (now Sri Lanka), sure that God was calling here there rather than to a destination in China where missionaries were usually sent for treatment. She realized that it would cause people to question her stability but concluded that "one must be content to be misjudged."[58]

In Ceylon, she found the three young missionaries she had gone to help had lost their older missionary coworkers to Malaria recently and had been praying for help. She set to work, evangelizing with them and learning the language, which came more quickly to her than Japanese had. Her health improved significantly, but she was warned she must not go back to Japan.

She received letters of objection to her hasty change of plans, a decision made on her own. Friends, her senior missionary in Japan, and Robert Wilson in England, objected and reproved her. She was a Keswick missionary. She had been warned not to join any other "mission house" (group of missionaries). Though their reactions disturbed her, still she felt God had led her to Ceylon.

Hearing that Eva, her sister, was preparing to be a missionary, she wrote her, "Practice balancing yourself on a pinpoint. It will be most useful."[59]

Remember that your missionaries will sometimes feel like they are balancing on a pinpoint as they seek to follow the Lord. Pray for wisdom for them as they do this balancing. Mission executives, families, coworkers will all give them advice and guidance and it should not be taken lightly. But missionaries must also consider their understanding of what the Lord is leading them to do. It was to Paul that the leading came to go to the Gentiles, though he did take great pains to explain it to the leaders back in Jerusalem.

---

[58] Sam Wellman, *Amy Carmichael: Selfless Servant of India* (Uhrichville, OH: Barbour Pub., 2012), pp. 69-73
[59] Ibid. p. 75-76

In November 1894, before her twenty-seventh birthday, Amy was making another radical adjustment as news came that Robert Wilson had suffered a stroke at the age of seventy. By the time she arrived home he was recovering, but she had no regrets about leaving Ceylon to be at his side. She considered him to be her second father.

It was he who encouraged her to publish her letters and magazine articles. It was at that time her first book, *From Sunrise Land*, came into print.

That winter she pondered her future. "In Japan she had failed as a missionary on two fronts. Her health was too fragile, and her facility for the language was lacking. But her stay in Ceylon had given her new hope. Perhaps there were places she could stay without being sickly. Perhaps there were languages she could master."[60] s

Before July of 1895, a letter from a friend serving in Bangalore, India, helped Amy, Robert Wilson, and her whole family to realize that South India would be a place that she could "get used to." The climate was mild, and the language was more agreeable. Again, she was saying her goodbyes.

Her place of ministry "full of lost souls who had never heard," was finally found, and she labored there until her death in January 18, 1951, at the age of eighty-three. But in that country, she still faced many adjustments to a culture full of disturbing, mysterious things, and wonders (read her book, *Things As They Are*) and to God's ways of using her.

For a while she traveled from place to place with her band of Indian coworkers, doing evangelistic work as she had in Japan and Ceylon. But soon they had gathered so many little girls rescued from Hindu temples where they had been dedicated to "the gods" that she realized they would have to settle down in one place in order to raise the children properly. It was just another adjustment she willingly made to what God was doing.

From that time on, looking after her rapidly growing family at Dohnavur in South India kept her busy and adaptable. Dohnavur

---

[60] Sam Wellman, *Amy Carmichael, Selfless Servant of India,* (Uhrichville, OH: Barbour, Pub. 2012), pp 77, 78

remains to this day a refuge for unwanted children and other outcasts of society where most have learned to trust the Jesus who loves them. Don't miss reading a full biography of Amy Carmichael.

PRAY...

- ...that your missionaries will remember well the process of their conversions and that it will continue to kindle in their hearts a desire to pray for and see many find that same rebirth.
- ...that the Lord will give them facility in language and perseverance to be always learning the strange pronunciations, nuances and idioms.
- ...that they will have wisdom to discern the Lord's guidance as they follow Him in the midst of sometimes conflicting advice.
- ...that they will be able to adjust to different cultures, changing circumstances, various types of ministries and roles, so that they can serve wherever the Lord leads them.
- ...that your missionaries will learn "to be content in whatever circumstances" in which they find themselves, *Philippians 4:11,* not only with regard to physical needs but in "every circumstance".
- ...that they will be sensitive to other missionaries as well as nationals making adjustments.

CHAPTER 9
~ ~ *Determination and Endurance* ~ ~

Henry Martyn

Determination and endurance are two important qualities for any missionary or Christian worker, and some have temperaments that include unusually larger quantities of these character traits.

Henry Martyn (1781–1812) as a boy was described as passionate, brave and constant, though slight, not very strong and fragile. He had a violent temper, which he worked hard to overcome, especially after he became a real believer.[61]

Henry sailed for India in 1805 as a chaplain of the East India Company. On the voyage, he applied himself to learning Hindustani,

---

[61] Basil Mathews, *The Book of Missionary Heroes* (USA: Pantianos Classics, 2016), L2280

Bengali, and Portuguese. He already knew Greek, Latin, and Hebrew.[62] His final destination was Cawnpore where he took up his post as chaplain.

In Kanpur (the spelling was changed from Cawnpore to Kanpur after India received its independence in 1946), a Christian Arab named Sabat was assigned to assist him, and soon Henry was able to converse with him in Arabic and Persian. Through Sabat's tales, Henry caught a vision for Mesopotamia, Arabia, and Persia.[63]

The New Testament had never been translated into good Persian, so Henry "slaved hard, far into the hot, sultry Indian nights, with scores of mosquitoes 'pinging' round his lamp and his head, grinding at his Persian grammar, so that he could translate the life of Jesus Christ into that language."[64]

> Even while he was listening to Sabat's story in the bungalow at Cawnpore, Martyn knew that he was so ill with tuberculosis that he could not live for many years more. The doctor said that he must leave India for a time to be in a healthier place. Should he go home to England, where all of his friends (and a sweetheart) were? He wanted that; but much more he wanted to go on with his work. He asked the doctor if he might go to Persia on the way home and the physician agreed.
>
> Martyn traveled across India from Cawnpore to Calcutta, and in a boat down the Hoogli river to the little Arab coasting sailing ship the *Hummoudi*, which hoisted sail and started on its voyage round India to Bombay. While on board Martyn read the Old Testament in the original Hebrew and the New Testament in the original Greek so that he might understand them better

---

[62] Ibid. L2294
[63] Ibid. L2311
[64] Ibid. L2319

and make a more perfect translation into Persian. He read the Koran of Mohammed so that he could argue with the Persians about it. And he worked hard at Arabic grammar, and read books in Persian. Yet he was ever cracking jokes with his fellow travelers, cooped up in the little ship on the hot tropical seas.

From Bombay, the governor granted Martyn a passage up the Persian Gulf in the *Benares*, a ship in the Indian Navy that was going on a cruise to finish the exciting work of hunting down the fierce Arab pirates of the Persian Gulf. So on Lady Day, 1811, the sailors got her under weigh and tacked up the Gulf, till at last, on May 21, the roofs and minarets of Bushire hove in sight. Martyn, leaning over the bulwarks, could see the town jutting out into the Gulf on a spit of sand and the sea almost surrounding it. That day he set foot for the first time on the soil of Persia.[65]

Aboard ship Martyn had allowed his beard and moustache to grow. In Bushire, he bought and wore the clothes of a Persian gentleman and rode out that night on his pony with an Armenian servant, Zechariah of Isfahan, on a 170 mile journey to Shiraz. They traveled by night to avoid the intolerable heat of the day. Still the heat was over 100 degrees. In the day, he pitched his little tent under a tree. He was already so ill that it was difficult to travel.

The heat rose to 126 degrees. Martyn could hardly sit upright on his pony. He used a wet towel wrapped around his head, which he said, "kept me alive, but would allow of no sleep."[66]

---

[65] Ibid. L2319-2329

[66] Basil Mathews, *The Book of Missionary Heroes* (USA: Pantianos Classics, 2016), L2338-2346

Then they went on climbing another range of mountains, first tormented by mosquitoes, then frozen with cold." Martyn was so overwhelmed with sleep that he could not sit on his pony and had to hurry ahead to keep awake and then sit down with his back against a rock where he fell asleep in a second, and had to be shaken to wake up when Zechariah, the Armenian mule driver, came up to where he was.

They had at last climbed the four mountain rungs of the ladder to Persia and came out on June 11, 1811, on the great plain where the city of Shiraz stands. Here he found the host, Jaffir Ali Khan, to whom he carried his letters of introduction. Martyn in his Persian dress, seated on the ground, was feasted with curries and rice, sweets cooled with snow and perfumed with rose water, and coffee.

Ali Khan had a lovely garden of orange trees, and in the garden Martyn sat. Ill as he was, he worked day in and day out to translate the life of Jesus Christ in the New Testament from the Greek language into pure and simple Persian.

As he sat there at his work, men came from hundreds of miles to talk with this holy man, as they felt him to be.[67]

At last they came to him in such numbers that Martyn was obliged to say to many of them that he could not see them. He hated sending them away. What was it that forced him to do so? It was because he was running a race against time. He knew that he could not live very long, because the disease that had smitten his lungs was gaining ground every day. And the thing that

---

[67] Ibid. L2363-2371

he had come to Persia for—was that he might
finish such a translation of the New Testament
into Persian that men should love to read years
and years after he had died.

He began the work within a week of reach-
ing Shiraz, and in seven months (February, 1812)
it was finished. Three more months were spent in
writing out very beautiful copies of the whole of
the New Testament in this new translation to be
presented to the Shah of Persia and to the heir to
the throne, Prince Abbas Mirza.

Again, he pressed on across Persia, enduring great fever and
many hardships, to find the Shah and the Prince and present the
good news of Christ in the New Testament to them. At last he
reached Tabriz and met the British Ambassador, Sir Gore Ouseley,
who said that he would deliver the precious cargo himself to the Shah
and Prince.

His great work was done. The New Testament was
finished. He sent a copy to the printers in India.
He could now go home to England and try to get
well again. He started out on horseback with two
Armenian servants and a Turkish guide. He was
making along the old track that has been the road
from Asia to Europe for thousands of years. His
plan was to travel across Persia, through Armenia
and over the Black Sea to Constantinople, and so
back to England.

For forty-five days he moved on—Yet he
was so ill that often he could hardly keep his seat
on his horse.

He travelled through deep ravines and over
high mountain passes and across vast plains. His
head ached till he felt it would split; he could not
eat; fever came on. He shook with ague. Yet his

remorseless Turkish guide, Hassan, dragged him along, because he wanted to get the journey over and go back home.

At last one day Martyn got rest on damp ground in a hovel, his eyes and forehead feeling as though a great fire burnt in them. 'I was almost frantic,' he wrote. Martyn was, in fact, dying; yet Hassan compelled him to ride a hundred and seventy miles of mountain track to Tokat. Here, on October 6, 1812, he wrote in his journal: "No horses to be had, I had an unexpected repose. I sat in the orchard and thought with sweet comfort and peace of my God—in solitude my Company, my Friend, my Comforter." It was the last word he was ever to write.

Alone, without a human friend by him, he fell asleep. But the book that he had written with his life-blood, the Persian New Testament, was printed, and has told thousands of Persians in far places, where no Christian man has penetrated, that story of the love of God that is shown in Jesus Christ.[68]

So what does this mean about our prayers for missionaries? Shall we pray that they will be careful to not kill themselves? Perhaps. Henry could have insisted that he be allowed to rest at intervals and not be driven to death. Maybe we should pray that they will have wisdom to know when to persevere and when to rest. After all, Henry had finished the task he was bent on doing. There was no need to rush.

A certain incident has often come back to me. It happened after an evening service in a church in Virginia where families brought their children to church Sunday evenings as well as Sunday morn-

---

[68] Basil Mathews, *The Book of Missionary Heroes* (USA: Pantianos Classics, 2016), L2388-2404

ings. A little girl of maybe eight years of age came up to me after we had given a report of the work and said, "I am going to be a missionary. And if I die I will go straight to heaven." I responded with, "That's right! Good for you." I was so touched by the faith of that child, who knew well that "greater love has no one than this, that one lay down his life for his friends" (John 15:13). We dare not say that Henry's sacrifice should not have been made.

When we first arrived on the field in 1965, all missionaries were required to sign a pledge yearly that, among other things, we would be willing to die for the Lord and for His work if necessary. It is well that we all commit to that at least once a year, whether we are on the mission field or at home. Let us pray for our missionaries (and for ourselves) that we remain willing to follow wherever He leads, even to death.

We will never understand in this life why God takes some of His servants home much sooner than we think He should. Sometimes we do see that the early death of some inspires many others to follow in service as in the case of the five young missionaries killed in the jungles of Ecuador in January 1956. Many missionaries trace their call to that event.

My friend from the nineteenth century, Annie, mentioned in the first chapter, died when her three children were still young. Her husband married two or three more times, losing each wife to death. I have read that single women in those days were tempted to think about which wife they might replace in case of her death. There were those in that century who arrived on the field and very soon went to bed and died of some disease or other.

There was a young man sent out to a mission station in the early 20th century. The senior missionaries on the station were able, after his arrival, to go on a well-earned furlough, confident that the mission was in his very capable hands. Imagine their grief when they received the news of the new missionary's tragic death in a hunting accident.

When we attended language school in the mountains above Dehra Dun, we were told of the student several years earlier who had slipped off of the mountain path while studying Hindi vocabulary cards as she walked along. She had fallen to her death. And there was the young missionary doctor in language school who was killed while fighting a fire near his home in the mountains.

We must simply trust that the Lord is in control and qualify our prayers for our fellow-workers with, "Nevertheless not my will, but yours, be done" (Luke 22:42). God's ways are not our ways and his thoughts not ours (Isa. 55:8–9; Eccles. 8:14).

Though it did not lead to death, I have seen much endurance of hardship among missionaries. David's father and his associates stood out in the hot summer sun of the plains day after day to draw crowds and preach the Gospel regularly. That was one of the methods of mission work at the time. Now even the nationals, as well as foreigners, are careful not to draw crowds out in the open so as not to attract persecution, though people are gathered freely in homes and other buildings still.

My need of endurance was with the cold in the winter. I could stay out of the hot sun in the summer, but the cold of the winter followed me wherever I went, even indoors where there is often no source of heat. Later, space heaters or wood fires in a stove or fireplace were used if we could afford the time to stay near them. The buildings had been built with high ceilings to keep cool in the summer. Therefore, in the winter, you could never heat a whole room.

So you can see that in our day we, especially I, did not endure very much real hardship, although there were times when I was struggling up mountain paths, trying to keep up with my family on outings, when I thought I was close to dying! But it was never the case.

Only once did I think of the words of Esther, "And so I will go—and if I perish, I perish!" That was when I had to merely cross a very wide, busy road in a large city, without any traffic signals or regulations as far as I could see.

I suppose David came closest to a "Henry Martyn experience" when we found our family high up in the Himalayas with him running a fever. When the day came to start down again, and he was still running a high fever, he just stood up and started down the path. I had no choice but to follow and pray. He made it.

I was there when David's dad took his last hike before he retired. I think it was down that same mountain path. He had picked up some stomach bug along the way. I was mostly leading that time, praying and squeezing lemons to mix with sugar water to keep up his strength. David was occupied, keeping track of the children's home boys and our children way ahead. It was too bad that sickness made it so hard for Dad on his last hike. He could normally hike circles around me.

Unfortunately, our culture has come to put so much emphasis on comfort that we tend to be "soft." Just the discomforts of normal living that people of a bygone age took for granted were hardships for people like me. But we are told to endure hardship (and I'm sure that means real hardship like beatings, being in jail, being hungry, etc.) like a soldier (2 Tim. 2:3). As far as I know, soldiers aren't able to think of their comfort. And I don't think Christ, whom we are supposed to be following, thought much about it either.

I must confess that I thought far too much of comfort in my missionary days. I sometimes described myself as a "wimp." I am extremely grateful that I was treated gently by the Lord and by my patient, loving husband and family. Some may remember that I did often mention things I thought uncomfortable (and amusing) in our prayer letters.

Pray…

- …that our missionaries will have balance in their lives as they serve. That they will neither be too comfortable (or even lazy) nor overzealous for the work, resulting in negligence of their welfare and that of their family.
- …that they will have the wisdom to discern whether the Lord is calling them to sacrifice their well-being, or even their lives, or if they should avoid doing so.
- …that they will understand what the real need is in getting the Gospel out to their targeted part of the world as Henry Martyn understood that the need of the Persian people was

to have the New Testament in their own language; that they will see clearly what their part is in meeting that need.

- ...that our missionaries, and all Christian workers, will be led to use their gifts, natural or spiritual, for the advancement of the Gospel just as Henry Martyn and many others did.

- ...that they will find great joy and satisfaction in serving with the gifts and opportunities granted them.

- ...that they will be faithful to the end, whether, in the providence of the Lord, their lives will be short or long.

- ...that the New Testament soon will have been translated into all languages.

CHAPTER 10
~ ~ Servant of All ~ ~

Edith and Francis Schaeffer

This chapter features a category rather than one particular missionary. The realization that she is in this category comes home clearly when a woman tries to fill in a form that asks for *occupation*. A missionary wife may be able to fill in "nurse" or "doctor" or "teacher," but if she hasn't worked professionally as such (though she may do a lot of nursing or teaching), that may not really fit. In that case, she will probably fill in "missionary wife," or since in most countries the "m" word is not used anymore, just "wife." I am grateful that I have never been asked to explain what that means exactly. It would be like when I am asked, "What do *you* do?" My first thought is, *Where do I begin?* and then all goes blank, and I can't think of a thing that I do that is worth telling.

The first time I wrote a Bible study, back in the eighties, on the biblical view of women, I called it *The Career of the Christian Woman.* It seemed to me that the world was putting the cart before the horse by urging all women to have "careers," meaning, in the case of the married women, something quite apart and beyond being wives and homemakers, raising and educating children, being hospitable, helping the poor, and investing time in the church.

The feminist definition of the word, "career" appeared, to be a profession for which women were paid that allowed them to use their gifts. The world, and unfortunately sometimes the church, influenced by feminism or egalitarianism, taught young women that they weren't adequately using their gifts by being good wives, mothers, or homemakers and assisting in their husbands' careers. They needed to have their own separate careers. The word, "gift," when Christians were teaching this, implied something spiritual as well as natural talents. Consequently, some wives were led to suspect that they were less than they should be spiritually if they didn't have a career by the world's standards.

Webster's definition of "career" is "calling pursued as a lifework." In the Bible study, I set out to demonstrate that this calling, or career, for the wife who desires to follow biblical principles is the one of the ideal wife of Proverbs 31:10-31. Though it was there, doing business was a very small part of her life. It was her husband and children who took front and center, and it was they whose opinions of her mattered in the end.

"Some may look down on the woman who spends most of her time caring for her family, but Christ said, "If anyone desires to be first, he shall be last of all and servant of all (Mark 9:35)."

One missionary wife who, I am quite sure, would agree with this statement, was Edith Schaeffer, wife of the well-known pastor, missionary, speaker and writer, Francis Schaeffer. She and her husband were contemporaries and friends of Frank and Esther Fiol, my husband's parents. Edith wrote books that inspired us, younger women, to use our gifts in helping our husbands and making our homes a center for ministry. She wrote widely-circulated family letters, describing how God was using the two of them in their combined calling and telling of the many lives that were being touched.[69]

Edith was providentially prepared well for her life's calling. She had lived with her missionary parents in China until she was five.[70] She felt a call at a young age to spend her life "making truth known."[71] She met Fran when he was twenty and she was seventeen at a church meeting in June 1932. They "overwhelmed each other," wrote the biographer. "For several years each had sought some companion of the opposite sex to talk to about the burning truth of Christianity."[72] Once again an Adam had been given a suitable Eve to assist him in doing God's work, and each had come to the commitment of putting God first, even before the other.[73]

They were married on July 6, 1935, after Fran graduated from college. They worked at a camp that summer, and Fran started studying at Westminster Seminary in the fall. Edith enjoyed it when Fran would run ideas past her, for she was very well versed in Christian doctrine.[74] The first of their four children was born in 1936.

After Fran's graduation from seminary in 1938, he pastored two small churches in Pennsylvania for two or three years each, and then they were called to the Bible Presbyterian Church in St Louis. All through their ministry, they emphasized evangelizing and training children and developed unique ways of doing it.

In 1947, following the war, the mission board of the Bible Presbyterian Church sent Fran to Europe to explore the possibility of doing evangelism there. He rejoiced in visiting the homeland of the reformers but discovered that the onrush of liberalism and the social gospel was even worse there than in his own country. The bible-believing churches of Europe appealed for help. After hearing

---

[69] Francis and Edith Schaeffe, *Evangelical Warriors, by Sam Wellman, Pillars of the Faith Series.* (Wild Centuries Press), L2368

[70] Ibid, L640-644

[71] Ibid, L722

[72] Ibid, L755

[73] Ibid, L941

[74] Ibid, L1112

his report, to his surprise, the Independent Board appointed him and Edith as missionaries to Europe to be there by February 1948.[75]

Thus began their missionary service in Europe that had far-reaching consequences and saw the establishment in 1955 of "L'Abri" (French for "the shelter").[76] The L'Abri model of ministry described in Edith Schaeffer's book, *L'Abri,* multiplied and has been used in the building of the kingdom in a number of countries. It was a place where many visitors were entertained and heard the Gospel. Fran would expound on secular culture from the Christian worldview. Ideas were discussed, not organizations, and many came to know the Lord.[77] Edith had a large part in this ministry as she used her many gifts, including hospitality and writing.

Edith's career was not an easy one. Early in their marriage, the faults of both of them became evident. Their biographer writes, "In fact, they had discovered they both had hot tempers. Edith reacted more often than Fran but usually with sarcasm. Fran reacted less often but more intensely, and with less self-control."[78] She had to be not only a suitable companion and helper intellectually but emotionally and temperamentally. She had to adjust herself to her husband's various ministries and spiritual struggles. At the same time, she had to nurture their four children and help them adjust to new cultures and the demands of their parents' activities.

Both Fran and Edith were caught in the turmoil of the small church that came out of the Presbyterian Church USA because of the latter's liberalism and desertion of the truths of the Word of God. The transition resulted in disagreements among leaders of the emerging Presbyterian Church of America, which led to the formation of a number of Presbyterian denominations. Eventually, in 1982, several of them, after merging, joined the Presbyterian Church in America. Perhaps as a result of this dissention and because his own church withdrew its support of their work at L'Abri, Fran was determined in

---

[75] Francis and Edith Schaeffer. *Evangelical Warriors, by Sam Wellman, Pillars of the Faith Series.* (Wild Centuries Press) L1520-1567
[76] Ibid, L1907
[77] Ibid, L1912
[78] Ibid, L1086-1091

his future ministry that discussions should revolve around ideas and not organizations.[79]

After starting his ministry in Europe, Fran became troubled by the caustic spirit generated by separation. The biographer writes:

> In his Bible-believing colleagues he saw little evidence of what the Bible said should be the results or "fruits" of belief. Instead of "love, joy, peace, patience, kindness, goodness, faithfulness, gentleness and self-control" promised by Paul in Galatians 5, Fran saw only contention, anger, and even hate. And these former fruits of the Spirit, which Fran thought he himself had possessed in abundance years ago after first becoming a Christian, he no longer felt. And yes, he too was full of anger. Where was love?[80]
>
> Though she felt no need to do it herself, Edith had to watch Fran rethink his faith from the beginning and come to the conclusion that, "—for the first time I see the basic answer. It is the thing for which I have been groping, I think. It is not less combat, but a *balance* between it and a real following the leading of the Holy Spirit—in short, a care that we do not minimize our personal spiritual lives.[81]

Balance in every area of life is something all wives and husbands struggle together to maintain. Edith and Fran faced it in the tension between time given to family on the one hand and other ministry on the other, as well as between the call to something new on the one hand and the duties already undertaken on the other. It often caused tension between them. Not only must each of a couple find the balance, but they must agree on the balance for each other. And through

---

[79] Ibid, L1911-1915
[80] Ibid, L1788-1800
[81] Ibid, L1795-1798

it all, the wives must be careful to be submitting to their husbands according to the instructions of Scripture, and the husbands must be careful to love their wives according to those same passages (Eph. 5:22–26; Col. 3:18–19; 1 Pet. 3:1–4). It is a matter for which our missionaries—and all of us—need prayer.

Edith had her own balance to maintain. On the one hand, she had the needs of her husband, which often meant caring for home and four children as well as the local work by herself when he was away on his many speaking engagements. On the other hand, she felt the call of many opportunities for ministry that she received and enjoyed.

Their son, who was five years old when L'Abri started, the youngest of their children, born seven years after their third daughter, did not do well.[82] Their son studied at a Boarding school in England. As a young boy, he contracted polio and was given much attention by his parents, but by the time he was coming into his early teens, Fran had become driven by a desire to reach more people than he could at l'Abri. He travelled far and wide to speak and wrote books, which made him even more in demand. He was away much more than Edith wished. The boy must have felt this tension and missed his father. Eventually, Edith saw Fran's viewpoint, and she also began traveling and speaking. They were not at L'Abri more than three months a year.

Edith Schaeffer and their children endured the sorrow of watching her husband die on May 15, 1984, at the age of seventy-two after a long battle with cancer. He had managed to finish his final book, *The Great Evangelical Disaster.* She lived on another twenty-nine years and died on March 30, 2013, at the age of ninety-eight.

We served under three agencies whose sponsoring denominations merged and successively accepted us. How grateful we are that the change in mission authorities came as a result of mergers of Bible-believing, evangelical and reformed Presbyterian churches, not splits.

Our mission boards had the policy for missionary wives that they should do only as much work outside of the home as they and

---

[82] Francis and Edith Schaeffer, *Evangelical Warriors, by Sam Wellman, Pillars of the Faith Series.* (Wild Centuries Press), L2013–2087, 2450–2462.

their husbands deemed best, for which we were extremely thankful. Other mothers at the international school, where our children attended, were able to be with their children at school only one or two months of the year since they were expected to hold down official jobs on their mission stations. If the couples felt the mother should be with the children more, it was not possible because of these responsibilities expected of the mothers.

All three couples of our mission were agreed that the mothers should live with the children close to the school so that they did not have to go into the school boarding. It was very helpful that our mission stations were within a fifty-mile radius so that the fathers could come up to the school on weekends or the mothers and children could go to the stations on weekends or during holidays.

Our location did not stop us mothers from keeping accounts and handling correspondence for the mission. And in addition, since we lived near the school, we mothers, and sometimes the fathers, also had a ministry with other students, in the local church and on committees of the board of the school. Putting our children first did not preclude ministry to others, it rather enhanced it.

We always considered our children to be our most important disciples. Setting that example for those around us was a vital part of displaying the love of God, our Heavenly Father. Wives who are involved in missions often find that caring for their children puts them in touch with women of the world concerned for their own children and open to hearing the Gospel and coming to Christ.

When our youngest was a senior in high school, I suggested that he might go into boarding so that I could live at a seminary with David and start to minister among women. Our son was well-established in his faith, and there was no fear that he would be led astray at that point. It might have been a good experience for him. But neither he nor my husband agreed to that plan. It was that year, when I stayed for one more year in the little cottage near the international school, that I was asked to lead a Bible study for women teachers and staff and wrote the course, "The Career of the Christian Woman." It had a significant impact on my life and future ministry.

One young woman from a distant area who had heard me at the seminary explain principles set forth in the Word for women, sent a message some time after she returned home, "Our society has been transformed." I could only guess how that happened as I had no further contact with her. Evidently obeying the Word of God had proved a blessing.

Kim Abernethy described so well the feelings of a Bible-believing missionary wife and the qualities of a Christian husband in the dedications at the beginning of her book, *In This Place*. She writes,

> To Jeff, my husband of 30 years: The vows we took all those years ago still resound in my heart. "Believing I was made for you only...." That said, God certainly knew I needed adventure in my life. Following you around the world has been extremely challenging, oftentimes difficult, and more times than not, simply amazing, but never boring. I love your heart for Christ. I love your quiet, but strong spirit. You are a spiritual leader in every way though I have not always appreciated that. Thank you for loving me unconditionally.[83]

Kim and her missionary pilot husband left for Liberia, Africa, under Baptist Mid-Missions in December 1985. Her book describes the thoughts, adjustments, and struggles of new missionaries in their first term in an African culture.

The Abernethys' intention, as with many career missionaries, was to minister at their first station for the rest of their missionary service. But an era of rebellion and war had come to the African continent, bringing an unsettling element to the missionary enterprise.

After one term of difficult but successful ministry for the missionary family, they returned happily to the people and the work they had become attached to for a second term. But the march of Charles

---

[83] Kim Lennon Abernethy, *In This Place: Cultural and Spiritual Collisions Refine the Heart of a Young Missionary in Liberia, West Africa* (Charlotte, NC: In Every Place Publishing, 2011).

Taylor's rebel army in the first year of that ministry made it impossible for them to continue. Read of the trials of that evacuation in the book, *In This Place*, by Kim Abernethy, available also in e-book format.

Kim's second book, *In Every Place*, describes their return to Africa, along with other displaced missionaries, on loan to Ivory Coast to minister to refugees from Liberia. She wrote, "Going into potentially dangerous and difficult circumstances was, to some of us, much better than not going at all. *Safety is of the Lord* and where he sends us, He is faithful to fulfill His perfect will."[84]

This book tells of even greater adjustments and trials than the first book does. They wore her down physically and emotionally, near to the breaking point for her and for their marriage. She endured fears, danger, and medical problems in the family, a husband often away on mission business and one more traumatic evacuation.

She confirms that, "Writing prayer letters at those times was exceedingly difficult. Saying just enough for prayer support, but certainly not painting the total picture. Missionaries in the trenches often do not believe people in American churches really want to know the whole truth of what we are facing in our ministries That may be an unfair assumption, but it does weigh on what we put in prayer letters sometimes." [85]

Often we are left to read between the lines if we want to do battle in prayer effectively because missionaries are not free to be specific for security reasons or for personal reasons. We can only imagine how we would feel in the circumstances they are in and spend time contemplating what we do know. We should remember that the situation is most likely much worse than they are describing and understand that they may not feel comfortable revealing in detail their inward struggles with the world, the flesh, and the devil.

It is no secret that suffering is a part of our lives in this world and especially as we are following Christ in obedience. Christ told us we are to take up our cross and follow Him (Luke 9:23). That sounds like suffering to me. The Apostles echoed the fact (Rom. 5:3; Rom. 8:17, 18; 2 Thess. 1:5; 2 Tim. 1:8, 2:3; Heb. 10:32).

---

[84] Kim Abernathy, *In Every Place* (Bethany Press International, n.d.) L225-230
[85] Ibid. L1048La

But praise the Lord, along with suffering is the promise for comfort (2 Cor. 1:5), growth (Rom. 5:3, 4), glory (Rom. 8:17, 18), and joy (1 Thess. 1:6; Matt. 5:11,12). Let us pray for comfort, growth, hope of glory, and joy in the face of suffering for our missionaries.

One of our major concerns should be for the relationships of husbands and wives as they strive to keep their marriages, which are a most important factor in their witness, biblical.

Pray...

- ...that mission boards will develop policies that will enable husbands and wives to make good choices for their marriages and for their children.
- ...that husbands and wives will be able to balance their lives in an agreeable way.
- ...that missionary wives will not feel pressured to center their activities outside of their families.
- ...that coworkers will be sensitive to the needs of each other's families.
- ...that all missionaries will be able to maintain a proper balance in every area of their lives.
- ...that missionaries will not be judgmental in the ways their fellow missionaries balance their lives.
- ...that the trials that come will not be more than they can bear and will not overcome the relationships of families.
- ...that your missionaries and their children as well will experience comfort, peace, hope of glory, joy, and growth in all of their trials.

Prayer Requests

CHAPTER 1

PRAY...

- ...for your missionaries' most serious trials and temptations, those they cannot express in letters. Pray that God will answer their prayers though they may not be free to reveal them to supporters.
- ...for the mission agencies, churches, and individuals who support them, that they will know how to pray, will take the time to do it, and will know what else they should do.
- ...that all family members will sense God's leading and mature in their spiritual lives as a result of the work to which their families have been called. Get to know each family member of your missionaries and pastors and their circumstances, and pray for each one regularly. Let them know how important they are in the work.
- ...for single missionaries who have families at home. Perhaps those families are concerned about their loved ones being on the field while single. The families at home, of both single and married missionaries, need prayer. Also intercede for your missionary's coworkers, that they will prove to be caring brothers and sisters in the Lord and will always look out for each other.
- ...that the Lord will enable your missionaries and their families to be inspired by the stories of others and to grow

in the faith that God works together difficulties, evil, and *all things* to accomplish His good purposes (Rom. 8:28).

- …that missionaries and supporters will understand that the greater the trials the greater the results for God's glory, both in Heaven and on earth, and the greater the results for the Kingdom, in us and in the work (James 1:2, 5:11; 1 Peter 1:6,7).

CHAPTER 2

PRAY…

- …that the work of Satan and his emissaries will be thwarted in the lives and ministries of those you are holding up. The promise is "Draw near to God, resist the Devil, and he will flee from you" (James 4:7).
- …that your missionaries, aware of their own weaknesses, will have the grace to work with the weaknesses and different points of view of their fellow workers, whether missionaries, or nationals.
- …that they will know when to go their separate ways in the face of ongoing lack of unity among co-workers.
- …that the Lord will give them the faith to believe through it all that truly for those who are serving the Lord, all things work together for good as promised in Romans 8:2.
- …that they may be enabled to always return good for evil, or what seems like evil to them.
- …that they, both missionaries and nationals, will have the Spirit of Christ who will help them love fervently, forgive their fellow workers and set an example of following Christ.

CHAPTER 3

PRAY...

- ...that the faith of your missionaries will remain strong.
- ...that they will learn more and more how to trust the Lord and walk by faith.
- ...that they will remember their call when problems and doubts come.
- ...that they will enjoy the important part of their ministry that takes place away from their field of service: visiting and reporting to supporters and raising prayer and financial support; offering people the opportunity to have a part in what God is doing.
- ...that their support and the resources needed for their special projects will come quickly.
- ...that they will have a good balance between quantity and quality in their work.

CHAPTER FOUR

PRAY...

- ...that your missionaries will have the faith to endure whatever trials God sends.
- ...that they will be aware of the power of the Holy Spirit working in and through them.
- ...that those to whom the missionaries are ministering will be able to hold them up in prayer at times when their faith and strength may falter, as the children prayed for Lillian in her time of weakness.
- ...that your missionaries will appreciate those upon whom they depend in the Lord's work, will regularly pray for them and encourage their supporters to do so as well.

- ...that the Lord will send capable, prayerful, faithful workers, both missionaries and nationals, to work alongside your missionaries.
- ...that your missionaries will not think more highly of themselves than they should or allow others to do so.

CHAPTER FIVE

PRAY...

- for discernment for your missionaries, that they be neither gullible nor cynical.
- that their own distinction between truth and falsehood will not be blurred.
- that they will never be found betraying the trust of anyone.
- that they "will be delivered from perverse and evil men;—." II Thes. 3:2
- that they will be protected in the midst of political turmoil or persecution and will have wisdom to know when to stay and when to flee.
- for grace for them to face whatever the Lord ordains for them.
- for the stability of the governments where they are working.
- That they will not be discouraged.

CHAPTER SIX

PRAY...

- ...that your missionaries will be able to raise their support quickly; that they will enjoy telling churches and individuals what God is doing and giving others opportunity to have a part in it through praying and giving.
- ...that they will have wisdom in investing money in the work with the goal of making it self-supporting.

- ...for wisdom for denominational authorities and mission boards as they make policies regarding missions, that they will be those that will give the support and guidance needed as the missionaries follow the leading of the Lord.
- ...for missionaries as they have differing ideas about the best methods of working, that they will respect each other and not be dogmatic.
- ...for occasions when such differences will necessitate a change in location or relationships, that it will be done quietly and cause as little disruption in the Lord's work as possible.
- ...that your missionaries and those guiding and supporting them will be dedicated to being peace-makers.
- ...that your women missionaries will know the joy and glory of being women following God's plan for womanhood as revealed in the Word of God.

CHAPTER SEVEN

PRAY...

- ...that your missionaries will understand how to extend that "horizontal grace".
- ...that they will have discernment to recognize the work of God in unusual ways in the nationals where they are working.
- ...that they will be able to discern also when they should distance themselves from methods that seem unscriptural.
- ...that the Lord will use nationals touched by your missionaries' work to reach other nationals whom missionaries could not influence.
- ...that your missionaries will themselves be and will allow others to be "all things to all men that they might by all means save some". (I Corinthians 9:22).
- ...that your missionaries will be prepared to suffer for Christ.

CHAPTER EIGHT

PRAY...

- ...that your missionaries will remember well the process of their conversions and that it will continue to kindle in their hearts a desire to pray for and see many find that same rebirth.
- ...that the Lord will give them facility in language and perseverance to be always learning the strange pronunciations, nuances and idioms.
- ...that they will have wisdom to discern the Lord's guidance as they follow Him in the midst of sometimes conflicting advice.
- ...that they will be able to adjust to different cultures, changing circumstances, various types of ministries and roles, so that they can serve wherever the Lord leads them.
- ...that your missionaries will learn "to be content in whatever circumstances" in which they find themselves, *Philippians 4:11*, not only with regard to physical needs but in "every circumstance".
- ...that they will be sensitive to other missionaries as well as nationals making adjustments.

CHAPER NINE

PRAY...

- ...that our missionaries will have balance in their lives as they serve. That they will neither be too comfortable (or even lazy) nor overzealous for the work, resulting in negligence of their welfare and that of their family.
- ...that they will have the wisdom to discern whether the Lord is calling them to sacrifice their well-being, or even their lives, or if they should avoid doing so.
- ...that they will understand what the real need is in getting the Gospel out to their targeted part of the world as Henry

Martyn understood that the need of the Persian people was to have the New Testament in their own language; that they will see clearly what their part is in meeting that need.

- ...that our missionaries, and all Christian workers, will be led to use their gifts, natural or spiritual, for the advancement of the Gospel just as Henry Martyn and many others did.
- ...that they will find great joy and satisfaction in serving with the gifts and opportunities granted them.
- ...that they will be faithful to the end, whether, in the providence of the Lord, their lives will be short or long.
- ...that the New Testament soon will have been translated into all languages.

CHAPTER TEN

PRAY...

- ...that mission boards will develop policies that will enable husbands and wives to make good choices for their marriages and for their children.
- ...that husbands and wives will be able to balance their lives in an agreeable way.
- ...that missionary wives will not feel pressured to center their activities outside of their families.
- ...that co-workers will be sensitive to the needs of each other's families.
- ...that all missionaries will be able to maintain a proper balance in every area of their lives.
- ...that missionaries will not be judgmental in the ways their fellow missionaries balance their lives.
- ...that the trials that come will not be more than they can bear and will not overcome the relationships of families.
- ...that your missionaries and their children as well will experience comfort, peace, hope of glory, joy and growth in all of their trials.

ABOUT THE AUTHOR

Eleanor and her husband, David, have worked in South Asia for about fifty years in the field of education and church planting. They presently live in Penney Farms, Florida.

She is a graduate of Covenant College and has been a writer since her high school days, finding great joy and help in processing life through writing letters, diaries, missionary prayer letters, and Bible studies as well as leading Bible studies and small groups for women. This book is one of the projects that God laid on her heart in retirement years. She is grateful to her husband, David, for his encouragement and editing assistance.

Eleanor and David have three grown children, eight grandchildren, and four great-grandchildren as of 2020.

CPSIA information can be obtained
at www.ICGtesting.com
Printed in the USA
FSHW011952260821
84347FS